"*Ready for PREtirement* is a comprehensive guidebook that covers everything you need to know about retirement planning. Author Kris Miller breaks down the big, scary money words into terms anyone can understand and provides the tools you need so you can get started immediately. Many people think retirement planning is just for seniors. But Miller taps into her vast estate planning experience to tell you why you should start planning NOW—even in your 20s, 30s, or 40s. Don't wait until it's too late. Follow Miller's advice and PREpare for PREtirement."

— **Danette Kubanda,** Emmy-winning television producer, writer and publicist

Praise for

READY *for* PRETIREMENT?

*Plan Retirement Early So Your Money is There
When YOU Need It*

"Do you have peace of mind that your money will be there when you need it? This insightful book is packed with inspiring 'can-use-it-today' forms and advice to set up a sound financial future so you can sleep at night with the knowledge that your golden years will truly be golden. Read it and reap."

— **Sam Horn,** The Intrigue Expert and author of *POP!*

"Kris Miller made a very complicated topic easy to understand and comprehend. She presents valuable information including step-by-step instructions on how to set up a personalized estate plan using today's volatile market to protect and increase an individual's assets. I highly recommend her services to all interested people curious about estate planning in general."

— **Debbie Carroll,** Executive Director, MusiCares,
The National Academy of Recording Arts & Sciences

"PREtirement, what an insightful way of putting it. Kris Miller, the Money Maestro, captivates, captures and provides the specific notes for your retirement song, which now can last a lifetime."

— **Robert Van Arlen,** International Speaker, Author and Business Strategist

"The information and services that Ms. Miller provides are extremely valuable to anyone who is considering structuring a living trust. As many of the Lions Club members are senior citizens, this information serves to protect the assets of our members and their families at a most crucial time."

— **Roland R.** Vellanoweth, President, Anza Valley Lions Club

"Kris Miller's informative material leaves anyone better prepared to face the problems we must all face sooner or later."

— **Jesse A. Edwards,** President, Murrieta Shrine Club

"As a lawyer who doesn't practice in this field, I wanted to find someone who worked in this field on a daily basis to advise me. Not only did I get my revocable living trust, I updated my life insurance, got a medical savings account and a long term care policy. I will recommend Kris Miller to others I know who are in need of her services."

— **Sam G. Vanderbrug,** Attorney at Law

"Retirement planning is a task we all must face—some of us sooner than others. Kris Miller has written an excellent book called *Ready for PREtirement?* It's a step-by-step guide that covers everything you need to know to get your finances in order. Miller takes an otherwise complicated process and breaks it down into steps that anyone can tackle. The book is packed with resources and worksheets that help you get started now so you can retire worry-free later."

— **Steve Harrison,** Radio-TV Interview Report (RTIR)

READY *for* PRETIREMENT

*Plan **Retirement** Early*
So Your Money is There
When YOU Need It

KRIS MILLER, CHFEBS, CSA, LDA

PREtirement
Plan Retirement Early

NEW YORK

READY *for* PRETIREMENT?

Plan Retirement Early So Your Money is There When YOU Need It

by KRIS MILLER, CHFEBS, CSA, LDA
© 2012 Kris Miller. All rights reserved.

ISBN 978-1-61448-125-6 Paperback
ISBN 978-1-61448-126-3 eBook
Library of Congress Control Number: 2011936720

Published by:
Morgan James Publishing
1225 Franklin Ave. Ste 325
Garden City, NY 11530-1693
Toll Free 800-485-4943
www.MorganJamesPublishing.com

Cover Design by:
Rachel Lopez
rachel@r2cdesign.com

Back Cover Design by:
Martha Bullen
writermb@verizon.net

Interior Design by:
Bonnie Bushman
bonnie@caboodlegraphics.com

In an effort to support local communities, raise awareness and funds, Morgan James Publishing donates a percentage of all book sales for the life of each book to Habitat for Humanity Peninsula and Greater Williamsburg.

Get involved today, visit
www.MorganJamesBuilds.com.

DEDICATION

Iam so thankful to have gotten close to my parents, especially in their later years. I found out what I didn't realize as a child. I never knew the quality of people I had been blessed to be brought up by until I had seen thousands of different family situations in my retirement/estate planning practice. My parents never compromised their principles, and their values were always based on the Good Book. They passed on those principles to me in loving and compassionate instruction. I saw my parents focus their attention, not just on the family, but also on helping others. Just as they generously gave to charity, I too have my favorite charities.

I dedicate this book to them as a token of my appreciation for all they have done for me.

ACKNOWLEDGMENTS

My mother's ten-year fight with cancer led me to share what I have learned through helping people develop their financial plans and living trusts. Watching my parents struggle with the same challenges my clients face was the inspiration I needed. As my mother kept smiling her way through the pain, and my dad kept loving and supporting her in every way he could, I knew that I could help others. Although watching my mother suffer was painful, I was also blessed. I knew that I could assist others in avoiding some of the monetary woes she had to endure.

I never really planned to write a book, but so many people have asked for this information that I decided to share these secrets in hopes that you, too, will share them with a friend.

I cannot begin to thank all the people who have helped me in writing this book. I can only thank God I have had so much encouragement from family and friends. I have been held in God's hand, nourished by the best parents anyone could hope for, and surrounded by legions of angels and friends who always show up at the perfect time to help.

I would never have been able to do what I am doing without the help and constant support of Lizzie, Joni, Debi, Annie, and Becky. And I was blessed with a wonderful "wordsmith." Sam Horn has taken all my pages and pages of words and brought them into clarity. By helping me realize who I have become over the last twenty years as a estate and living trust expert, she has helped me to merge that financial expertise with the deeper love of God which I have always expressed in song—songs that are now playing around the world.

I am also especially thankful for Barbara NcNichol, the editor who has organized all my years of experience into a readable format. Phyllis Oscar also offered helpful suggestions with a final read-though of the project. Danette Kubanda, thanks for your amazing input and help. You are a joy to work with. Victoria St. George of Just Write, thanks for your careful and thorough proofread—you made this book better! Mike Koenigs, Pam Hendrickson and Chris Hendrickson, thanks in advance for all your help and advice and great Mastermind group..

Martha Bullen, copywriter and publicity consultant for Bradley Communications and managing editor of Book Marketing Update—I appreciate your help with the back cover. Mary Agnes Antonopoulos, Social Media Master, you are an angel. Brad Codd, I appreciate your kindness and look forward to the best teleseminar series, "Are You Ready for PREtirement?" Brandon Frank, you are the best IP attorney and I appreciate your watching my back. Tom Antion, you are the best marketer with the best programs. Your kind heart is a plus. Stefanie Hartman, thanks for all your great tips. Alex Mandossian, I appreciate your Mastermind group. And I received lots of help from my friends. I will not have enough paper to include your individual contributions. Also thanks to Steve Harrison for your positive support, Geoffrey Berwind for your great content and good heart, and Raia King for your much appreciated content and contacts. Rick Frishman and David Hancock for helping me with all the details of publishing. And the cherry on top Ben Neumann, who is taking my marketing to the next level.

Above all, I am grateful to God, who gave me the faith to complete this project and the hope that it will help many, many people.

CONTENTS

Dedication vii

Acknowledgments ix

Introduction 1

The Unexpected Emotional and Financial Cost of the
Death of a Loved One 3

Let's Begin: Are You *Ready for PREtirement*? 4

Financial Security: Will Your Money Be There When You Need It?............... 5

What You Will Learn In This Book 5

Chapter 1: PREtirement Now—What Does It All Mean? 7

Responding to Our Biggest Challenges 9

Challenge 1: Being Part of the Sandwich Generation 9

Challenge 2: Dealing with an Unexpected Catastrophic
Illness and Long Term Care 10

Challenge 3: Families and Money 12

Challenge 4: Social Security and Taxes 13

Challenge 5: Estate Planning Decisions
and How They Affect Your Family and Friends 13

Challenge 6: The Stock Market Myths that Just Won't Die 17

Challenge 7: Having Funds for a Secure and Comfortable Retirement......... 23

Your Relationship With Money 25

**Chapter 2: Retirement Planning—The Living Trust and
Your Estate Planning Decisions** 31

Take Control of the Estate Planning Process 32

The Difference Between A Will and a Trust... 33

Naming a Personal Representative 34

Naming a Guardian for Your Minor Children....................................... 37

Specific Distributions.. 39

Marital Concerns... 40

Children's Shares—Creation of Trust for Minor
             and/or Adult Children 41
The Common Trust 42
Terms of the Child's Trust 43
"Special Needs Trust" for a Disabled Child 44
Ultimate Distributions 45
Naming a Trustee 47
Initial Trustees 49
Successor Trustees 50
Powers of Attorney 51
When Should the Power of Attorney Become Effective? 53
Your Living Will 54
Artificially Provided Food and Water 55
Organ Donation 55
Time for Changes: PREpare for PREtirement 56
Estate Planning Tools for Charitable Giving 57

Chapter 3: Long Term Care Options—Protection of Assets 65
Option 1: Purchase Insurance 66
Option 2: Protect Your Nest Egg—Buy an Annuity 68
Option 3: Set Up a Reverse Mortgage 70
State and Federal Government Intervention 70

Chapter 4: Medicaid Planning—Entitlement Programs 73
What is Medicaid? 75
What Is Covered by Medicaid? 75
Applying for Benefits 78
Medical Qualification Rules 82
Income Qualification Rules 82
Asset Qualification Rules 90
Married: Community Spouse Resource Allowance (CSRA) 97
Transferring Assets (Gifts) 103
Estate Recovery 108

Chapter 5: Financial Legacy and the Excellent PREtirement Choice 117
No Risk, Just Reward 118
The Top Three Myths of Financial Planning 120

Summary and Plan of Action 125

About Kris Miller, ChFEB, CSA, LDA 127

An Invitation from Kris Miller 129

Appendix Contents.. 131

    Appendix A   Organization of Documents................................ 133

    Appendix B   Revocable Living Trusts 137

    Appendix C   Checklist of Activities After a Death 141

    Appendix D   Documents Checklist.. 143

    Appendix E   Personal Information and Funeral Plans 145

    Appendix F   Assets and Possessions 149

    Appendix G   Family Medical Information 153

PREtirement Glossary.. 157

Helpful Internet Resources for Retirees, Aging Adults, and Caregivers........ 167

INTRODUCTION

I can still smell the chocolate chip cookies in the oven. Mom would allow me to have two cookies if I cleared the table and cleaned the dishes. But the urge to run out and play with my friends pulled stronger than the deal offered by my mom. Before I could get out the front door, she would be calling me back into the kitchen with that loving but no nonsense look in her eye. She handed me a dishtowel. No way was she letting me skip out on the dishes.

Not only did my dad always spend time with me on algebra, math and spelling, but when I was in junior high and wanted to build an electric motorcycle, my dad worked on it with me every weekend. My mom and I would make bread in tin cans which I would take with me when I rode my minibike (which was a 3½ hp Briggs & Stratton lawn mower) across the rolling hills in the rain with the muddy water splashing in my face. She set me up with every creative art project she could think of, either showing me how to complete it herself, or finding someone who could teach me.

As you can tell, I loved my parents and appreciated the childhood they provided for me. That's probably why it was so very difficult when my mom was diagnosed with cancer 50 years later. Unlike the dinner dishes my dad and I could skip out on, we had to face the responsibilities that came with mom's illness. We couldn't run away from the emotional tidal waves and unexpected burdens during the painful and anxiety-filled years of her illness.

After having an ideal relationship with my parents, I didn't anticipate what became a very challenging time, primarily because we hadn't prepared adequately for Mom's unexpected medical expenses. Our emotional devastation was compounded by the volume and variety of legal and financial complications we faced.

On the second day after my mother's cancer operation, she was moved from the Intensive Care Unit into a nursing home. Hospitals follow the three-day diagnosis-related group (DRG) rule or the 72-hour rule. This means that all services provided for Medicare patients within 72 hours of the hospital admission are considered part of the inpatient services and are to be billed on one claim. Therefore, as a way to reduce their costs, hospital administrators want to release patients quickly and usually send patients to convalescent homes, often before they are ready.

Did you know that?

Later on, my mother shared her treatment bills with me, hoping what I learned from deciphering them could be used to help others. As an example, the bill for the five-day chemotherapy treatment she took every month was $90,000, and she had treatments 12 months in a row. That adds up to $1,080,000 for *only the chemotherapy.* That doesn't include other drugs, therapies or doctors.

Did you know that?

My parents came from the generation who thought Social Security would always be there and their pensions would last forever. Not true! Can you imagine all the years they paid into Social Security, thinking it would be there when they needed it, and then finding out the funds weren't available? After the first twenty days that Medicare covered "free," my mother's co-payment was close to $10,000 a month. Medicare does not cover nursing home care for more than 100 days a year.

Did you know that?

Oh by the way, the hundreds of thousands of dollars in medical bills meant my dad had to postpone retirement. And now, at 92, he's still paying down the bills.

The Unexpected Emotional and Financial Cost of the Death of a Loved One

It wasn't until I became a paralegal and volunteered at a senior center that I learned the secrets that many attorneys and court officials aren't telling you. They may tell you how to draw up a will but they won't tell you:

- how to avoid probate
- how to select a trusted conservator
- that the probate process often takes years to be resolved and can lead to a loss of from 4 percent to 20 percent of your estate's value, depending on state court costs and fees
- how to invest your money in safer, less risky options so it will last through your senior years

What really bothers me is seeing widows (not only 80-year-old widows, but 35-year-old widows) who have no money left after they lose a loved one. Even the house they owned can become state property if they don't have the right paperwork.

After going through this nightmare with my own family—the same experience that millions of other Americans go through every year—I realized that something should be done. And then I thought that I could be the one to do it!

I developed a program that makes it easy for the average person to understand the critical information that affects their finances. Initially, I titled my program the *Living Trust Workshop* and the *Senior Survival Workshop.* I have since renamed it the *PREtirement Survival Workshop.* The workshops aren't just for retirees or people over the age of 65. In fact, if you're working, have a retirement plan or support a family member, then this book is for you.

Will your money be there when you need it? Let's be honest, your salary can only go so far—especially when you have a lot of expenses to pay, like monthly bills, food and emergencies. So how can you save for retirement?

Go to the following link to download *"How To Save For Retirement,"* for five options you can use to start saving now.

http://krismillermoneymaestro.com/saveforretirement
Learn more at: http://ReadyForPREtirement.com

Let's Begin: Are You *Ready for PREtirement?*

PREtirement: *Noun.* 1. The act of preparing early for retirement. 2. Planning ahead to avoid probate, long term care and the Great Recession and making sure your money lasts as long as you do. 3. P = Plan, R = Retirement, E = Early. 4. PRE-plan before you are *tired*.

The PREtirement plan provides the following benefits:

- protects your assets from catastrophic illness and nursing home costs
- earns more interest on your money with depression-proof safety
- lowers or eliminates taxes on Social Security and interest income
- moves your 401(k) or IRA without cost so you can afford to retire

For the past two decades, I have given workshops around California 10 months a year. I am eager to break the stranglehold of attorneys gouging people for thousands of dollars when all they need is a simple yet comprehensive estate plan. Some people with complex situations may require intricate and expensive estate planning, but many of us can reach our planning goals with the information contained in this book, with or without the targeted assistance of an attorney or qualified estate planner. Although I charge a fraction of what most attorneys and paralegals charge to prepare the documents for living trusts, wills and powers of attorney, I have acquired a reputation for dealing with my clients with integrity and compassion. As the word about my work has spread, my practice has grown, enabling me to keep my fees affordable.

During my 20 years as a retirement and estate planner, I've seen too many people lose their money or homes as a result of unanticipated health crises that led to accompanying astronomical catastrophic bills. What I have learned is something I rarely see reported elsewhere. In fact, I believe that the laws on Medicaid, or MediCal as it's known in California, are intentionally confusing so that most people can't understand them. In many cases, people are forced to hire a professional to get the benefits they are qualified to receive.

This unacceptable situation gave me a mission. This mission was to make my workshops and books understandable to the "everyday person." I want people to ask questions and take away details that will help them get their affairs in order. This book will enable readers to create a comprehensive estate plan, regardless of their age or situation.

You'll see that this book is packed with specific rules, regulations, policies and their exceptions. Though you may feel overwhelmed by all the forms and the time needed to gather the information to complete the documents, please do not give up. It's easier than you think.

Remember, you will have to do this preparation someday… and sooner is better than later. Investing a few hours now with a pen in your hand will make a substantial difference because it can prevent your hard-earned money from being taken away from you. I guarantee it will be time well spent. Why? Because it is in your best interest to make my motto your motto: *PREpare for PREtirement.*

Financial Security: Will Your Money Be There When You Need It?

This book captures hands-on knowledge I've accumulated from working with thousands of clients. While you won't find a customized consultation for your situation on these pages, you will find examples of circumstances that are similar to yours. I've gathered a range of data and scenarios to help you make more informed decisions for you and your loved ones.

In counseling more than 5,000 families, I've concluded that 90 percent of people simply aren't prepared for their financial future and the health issues that they will eventually have to confront. Wouldn't you rather have peace of mind by preparing now?

By following the advice in this book, you and your loved ones won't be left with regrets and astronomical bills. Using the strategies I recommend, you'll be protecting your hard-earned assets so they will be available when you need them. Grab your pen. Let's begin.

What You Will Learn In This Book

Here are a few of the questions addressed throughout this book:

- How can your money be safer in a down market?
- How can you protect your principal and still grow your money?
- How can you put a "bottom" on your money and not lose principal?
- How can you avoid probate and long term care costs so your money lasts as long as you do?

- Will your "bucket list" leave you singing the blues?
- How will you pay for an unexpected catastrophic illness, accident, or tragic event such as a child's sports injury, a vacation mishap, or a natural disaster?
- Why is it advisable to create a living trust?
- How can you avoid probate, keep your affairs in order, and protect your assets from court fees and disgruntled heirs?
- If your nest egg is cracked, what can you do about it?
- Will you lie awake wondering if you'll have money for retirement?
- Why won't most people talk to a financial advisor?
- How can you earn more interest on your money with depression-proof safety built in?

I constantly pose these questions to my clients, depending on their needs. In my sessions and workshops, I love to share what's called an "Estate of Mind." It refers to the peace of mind you'll have knowing you've done your best for your own and your family's future. It occurs automatically when you start PREtirement planning.

PREtirement planning keeps you one step ahead and changes with age. Just like a song, the beat changes and so must your planning—to keep up with changes in your income, health and family situation.

I'm an expert in tax-deferred programs that allow you to withdraw an income and still be guaranteed to have money left for a spouse or heirs, regardless of what happens to the market or interest rates. That is why I'm proud to say my clients love me. I have never lost one dollar of their money. They say I'm "in tune" and have given me the nickname "money maestro."

My clients don't lie awake wondering if they'll have money left for retirement or if they'll outlive their savings. I have shown them how to take distributions from an IRA over their life expectancy and still guarantee to leave them more money than they've ever deposited for any beneficiary, regardless of interest rates or market.

Make my motto yours: "Expect the unexpected; be PREtirement ready."

www.ReadyForPREtirement.com/

Chapter 1

PREtirement NOW—
WHAT DOES IT ALL MEAN?

"Begin with the end in mind."
— **Stephen R. Covey**

PREtirement means being PREpared for the future!

When Sue and Bob, a couple I counseled, recently turned age 65, they went to get their pensions, only to discover their funds had disappeared with the downturn of the market. Despite having lost almost everything in the market, their broker still wanted them to invest their last remaining IRA funds in the stock market (no doubt without explaining the risk). When they questioned this strategy, the broker became defensive. They tried to contact him to ask him specific questions, but he never returned their calls.

Without their pensions, Bob and Sue are facing a very uncertain future. They will probably be eating peanut butter and jelly sandwiches in their golden years and working some part-time jobs. They didn't PREpare for the unexpected.

Don't be caught unaware as Bob and Sue were. This chapter will introduce you to the most common financial situations that will arise at various stages of your life. But first, to get you started, I want you to consider the following questions:

1. **Are you ready to handle an unexpected financial crisis?**
2. **Do you have a will and have you taken steps to protect your assets so they will be distributed according to your wishes?**
3. **What does Social Security really cover?**
4. **Have you invested money according to your age and risk tolerance so that you will have a financially secure retirement?**

If you haven't spent time managing your finances, making these decisions can seem overwhelming. But the fact is that you will end up paying perhaps a significant sum of money unnecessarily if you don't begin to address these issues now. It's not just that you could lose money by choosing the wrong investment vehicles. You could be paying costly premiums on an insurance policy that doesn't provide the coverage you need or want. By starting now to keep your finances in order, you will be protecting yourself and your family for the future. Don't put it off. Whether you're investing for retirement, setting aside an emergency fund for the unexpected or estate planning, PREpare: be proactive and start today!

A number of documents will help you get started. I give my PREtirement clients comprehensive forms to organize documents, to compile data that goes into revocable living trusts, and to make a step-by-step checklist for actions they need to take following the death of a loved one. Yes, I have given these valuable documents to you, too, in the Appendix. *Please remember, though, that these forms are for general use in many situations and may not cover your specific circumstances. If you have any questions or think you want to change the forms significantly, that is probably a sign that you should consult with an estate planning professional.*

Responding to Our Biggest Challenges

Challenge 1: Being Part of the Sandwich Generation

What is the Sandwich Generation? It's a relatively new phrase, but one now included in the latest editions of *Oxford English Dictionary* and *Webster's Collegiate Dictionary*. It's the demanding time when people are coping simultaneously with their growing children and their aging parents, while thinking about their own retirement. Deciding which has the highest priority can tear a marriage—or an individual—apart.

An estimated 25 percent of the American population is classified as the Sandwich Generation, meaning they are parenting their own children and taking care of their parents at the same time. Some estimates show that nearly two-thirds of the baby boomer generation will be taking care of an elderly parent in the next ten years. As the Sandwich Generation grows, the need to understand aging dynamics and family relationships increases dramatically.

It's not easy to become elderly or a parent to your parent(s). After all, society believes adults should be able to take care of themselves. But as more people live well into their 80s and 90s with their families dispersed across the country, everyone will be involved in some way in elder care—if not today, then tomorrow.

You may take some comfort in knowing that you are not alone. You now have a new role on the stage of life, for which you can never rehearse. Currently, the typical American Sandwich Generation caregiver is in her mid-40s, married, employed and caring for her family and an elderly parent, usually her mother. But, more and more men are finding themselves in a caregiving role. Many are in rural areas, with very limited access to such resources as senior centers, or even Meals on Wheels. Many of these couples face major stress in their finances, emotions, and relationships. What happens to a couple's dreams for slowing down, with a secure retirement and a chance to travel?

Any parent knows that taming an active two-year-old can be a full-time job. But caring for an elderly parent as well can be overwhelming. Mrs. S. was not only taking care of her grandchildren, she was also caring for her mother, a formerly active 75-year-old who had been harmed by toxic side effects of a prescription drug and now needed full-time care. Mrs. S. was so busy that her husband moved out. She had never imagined such problems! With her daughter having to work two jobs to provide for her family, there was no end in sight. Then we talked and helped her find a way to improve the family situation in the short term.

We were able to roll her IRA, which had lost 40 percent in the market, into an equity index annuity with income. That way she was able to have more income and be able to help her daughter. Among other suggestions, I told her whom to contact so her mom could go to the senior center where they have an elder day care program. Now her mom can hang out with other seniors and play bingo at no cost while Mrs. S. works.

Challenge 2:
Dealing with an Unexpected Catastrophic Illness and Long Term Care

My 20-year-old niece was a straight-A student, star of her class, attending Boston University on scholarship. A perfect beauty in great health, she was an up-and-coming theater star. One day during vacation, she fell into a coma for no apparent reason. I'll never forget seeing her in the hospital bed, surrounded by her friends singing and holding her hand. It's one of those situations that you cannot imagine until it actually happens to you. There were so many conflicting emotions, so much uncertainty about whether she would ever wake up. It was so hard on everyone to feel so helpless.

And then, in the midst of all that emotion, the practical questions arise: What if she stays in a coma? Who will take care of her? How would her parents be able to care for her if they need to work full-time? How much would health insurance pay—if anything—to cover a convalescent stay? Sadly, my niece died shortly after becoming ill and her parents didn't have to deal with these issues. But how would you PREpare for this kind of situation?

Another client, age 39, was running on a treadmill when his iPod slipped off the machine. He reached down and fell, hitting his head and sustaining a brain injury that has left him incapacitated. His wife works full-time; they have three kids and a mortgage. His insurance doesn't cover the kind of care he needs.

In addition to all the emotions and the financial worries, you need to consider the legal issues when someone is unable to voice their preferences for care. Remember the case of 26-year-old Terri Schiavo of Florida. She certainly didn't anticipate slipping into a coma in 1990 and then having her husband and parents fight over her medical care and her ultimate wishes for the next 15 years.

Planning for medical emergencies is a must for everyone and should include the signing of two important legal documents: a living will and an advance medical directive. Make sure that your directive includes language that satisfies the federal HIPPA (Health Information Privacy and Portability Act) law or your medical records cannot be released to the people you want to make health care decisions for you when you cannot. If you are out of the country on business and your spouse is at home trying to sell the house, or if you are in an accident and expected to fully recover but will be in the hospital for a while, then you will also need a durable power of attorney to allow your spouse or another person of your choice to manage your finances and sign legal documents on your behalf.

And what about long term care? Today, 20 percent of people under age 65 and 70 percent of seniors over age 65 in the U.S. will end up using convalescent care, home health care, custodial care, intermediate care or respite care. Given the statistics, nursing home residency could well be in your own future. And it's unlikely that Medicare or Medicaid will cover these costs. That's why two-thirds of married people and one-half of single people will end up in bankruptcy within 13 weeks of entering a nursing home. Monthly costs average $6,000 to $15,000 without including medical expenses and drugs. With only 10 percent of people over age 65 in the U.S. today having long term care insurance, it's not uncommon for people to go into bankruptcy as they help care for their elderly parents. You may find that you're drawing on your savings, retirement plans, home equity line of credit or credit cards.

If you're young and healthy, you probably can't imagine that you would ever need long term care. Even if your parents are older, you may not want to envision them in less than perfect health. But sticking your head in the sand on this subject is just foolish.

Obviously, you need to do serious—and advance—planning, knowing that you'll be responsible for most of your long term care expenses. To protect your assets when dealing with medical "spend-down," your options include long term care (LTC) insurance, which pays some or all costs of nursing home care for those who qualify, modified endowment life insurance, which is payable to the insured if he or she is still living on the policy's maturity date, or government-funded Medicaid planning, which pays for medical care for low-income individuals. These and other long term care preparations are discussed in more detail in chapter 3.

One of my clients, Frank, was 92 years old. He was in great shape and had just driven from California to Montana where he fixed up and resold mobile homes. He also took care of a neighbor who had dementia. When his wife, Betty, got Alzheimer's, he took care of her for as long as he could until he couldn't lift her anymore. He now visits her in a nursing home every day, but she doesn't recognize him.

One day, he said, "Kris, I was never told Medicare won't cover all your convalescent care in a nursing home and at home." But it doesn't, and Frank learned that through firsthand experience. He's forced to pay for Betty's care by spending down their estate. It took them years of careful saving and "doing without" to end up with enough money to see them through their final years together. Or so they thought. With all the expenses they have to cover for Betty's care, their painstakingly built retirement fund will be depleted in a year.

Frank thought he'd give some of his money away so Betty could get on Medicaid, but there's a five-year "look-back" period. So he'd have to wait for another five years before applying for Medicaid or face misdemeanor charges. That's yet another reason why it's important to do your PREtirement planning now!

Challenge 3: Families and Money

If you are young and in love and don't think that you need to plan for retirement before marriage, think again. For example, many circumstances warrant the consideration of a prenuptial agreement, including being involved in a family-owned business, owning your own business, having a substantial 401(k) or other retirement plan, inheriting assets from your family, owning a residence that will be used as the marital home, or marrying someone who has already accumulated a large amount of debt. A prenuptial agreement can protect what assets you currently have or significant assets that you expect to inherit, and can also protect your assets from the debts your partner acquired before marriage.

If you have minor children, estate planning is a necessity, not just for financial reasons. You will need to name a Guardian to take care of your children (more about this in Chapter 2). Without a plan in place, if both you and the other parent of your children die while the children are still minors, then the children will become wards of the court until a judge can decide with whom the children should live until they become adults. Without a plan in place, control of the minor's inheritance will be taken over by a court-supervised Guardian or Conservator whose fees will be paid for out of the inheritance. Then, depending on the laws of the state where the minor lives, when the child reaches the age of 18 or 21, whatever guardianship funds may remain will be turned over to the young adult, with no guidance, supervision, or accountability. They may be fine—or it may be a disaster. Through proper PREparation, you can make advance decisions that you feel are best in your particular circumstances and write documents that will allow you to express those decisions and preferences.

Challenge 4: Social Security and Taxes

President Franklin Delano Roosevelt set up Social Security in 1935 to help Americans have an income or pension after age 65. While FDR probably didn't intend to have older people taxed on their earnings in their senior years, that's essentially what happens today. Therefore, you should consider some of the following strategies to reduce your taxes.

Giving can reduce taxes. Gifts in any amount between spouses are tax-free. Gifts are never taxed to the donor. Current gift tax laws also permit gifts of $13,000 per year, per individual, to any number of recipients with no tax consequences. Also, any direct payment of medical and education expenses on behalf of another escapes taxation. Making gifts now can reduce the size of your estate and potentially reduce estate taxes upon your death. If the gifts are to charitable institutions, such gifts can also reduce your income taxes in amounts that vary, depending on your income.

Shift your income into tax-exempt securities. You can put money into municipal bonds, for example.

Consider the tax consequences of working or not working. I know that I've said that you may not have enough money saved to live comfortably, especially if you have larger than anticipated medical bills. But you need to consider carefully whether working will end up costing you more money than not working because you'd end up paying taxes and potentially becoming ineligible for certain benefits.

Challenge 5: Estate Planning Decisions and How They Affect Your Family and Friends

What did Heath Ledger, Marilyn Monroe, Michael Jackson, John Wayne, Jacqueline Kennedy Onassis, Princess Diana, and Anna Nicole Smith have in common? They all had lousy wills. Because of this, their deaths left not just emotional turmoil for their friends and families, but also financial uncertainty, legal battles, and expensive, long term, court-ordered supervision of the estates, which drained the assets away from the people whom they wanted to benefit.

These are famous people with lots of money. But no matter your net worth, it's important to have a basic estate plan in place. Such a plan ensures that your family's financial goals are met after you die. This is essential if you have young children or elderly parents whom you support.

Did you know that, without a living trust, your financial legacy could end up in probate, with your estate's assets being controlled and eventually eaten up by lawyers and court fees? On the other hand, with proper planning, you could have a document that ensures your estate passes to your heirs without delays or time- and money-consuming probate. You can name someone you trust to take care of your estate so you know everything you worked to accumulate will transfer at death according to your wishes.

You should take steps to ensure that someone you trust will be able to take care of your personal, health and financial decisions if you are unable to do so. In the absence of any formal estate planning, the court will decide who will take care of you and your financial affairs, and might appoint someone you would not have chosen.

If your financial life is simple and straightforward, you may feel comfortable creating your estate plan by yourself. If you have multiple bank and investment accounts, real estate investments, or a nontraditional family situation, you may well want to consult with a lawyer.

Before you meet with an attorney to draft a will, consider the following.

Taking inventory of your assets is a good place to start. Your assets include your bank and other investment accounts (such as money market or mutual funds), retirement savings, insurance policies, and real estate or business interests. Ask yourself three questions: (1) Whom do you want to inherit your assets? (2) Whom do you want handling your financial affairs if you're ever incapacitated? (3) Whom do you want making medical decisions for you if you become unable to make them for yourself?

Trusts aren't just for the wealthy. Trusts are legal constructs that let you put specific conditions on how and when your assets will be distributed upon your death. They also allow you to reduce your estate and gift taxes and to distribute assets to your heirs without the cost, delay and publicity of probate court, which administers wills. Some trusts also offer greater protection of your assets from creditors and lawsuits.

Discussing your estate plans with your heirs may prevent disputes or confusion. Inheritance can be a loaded issue. By being clear about your intentions, you help dispel potential conflicts after you're gone. It shocks me every time I see people fight over the material things in their own families, but it happens all the time. I had a client who not only sued the estate of the uncle who left him a portion of his estate, but also sued every other relative to get more from the estate. His family members were amazed. They never saw it coming until they were served papers.

A will is not enough. A will, written and signed properly, directs "who's in charge" and "who gets what" from your assets at the date of death, but it's of no use before you die. If you become incompetent, it doesn't control your assets or designate who can make health care decisions for you. After you die, a will doesn't avoid probate of your estate. In fact, a will can be a one-way ticket to the fees and delays of probate court.

Make sure you fund your trust. We advocate for the use of trusts as a useful tool to manage your assets during your life and following your death, avoiding the time and expense of the probate court. Trusts, however, only manage those assets that you actually, officially transfer into trust. Once your trust is complete, be sure to transfer your assets into it. For assets with a legal title, such as real property and automobiles, you have to change the title to the name of the trust (although in some states you can keep the car registered in your name but use a "transfer on death" title so that the car is automatically registered to the person you name on the title). For nonretirement accounts, you can simply contact your bank or the portfolio manager of your accounts and request that they change the title on your accounts from your name to the name of your living trust (some banks have accounts that are "payable on death" to a specific beneficiary). For assets with no legal title, such as household goods, you simply include them in the list of trust assets in a "schedule" at the back of the trust document.

Keep your papers in a safe place. Make sure your Successor Trustee and the person who holds your power of attorney know where you are going to keep these documents and how to get to them. You can put them in a safe deposit box, but make sure the Successor Trustee and Power of Attorney have signed the signature card and have a key. A health care power of attorney is only useful if the document can be accessed when needed, so it's a good idea to give the Power of Attorney his or her own copy, but make sure the original signed papers are in a safe place.

Designate a health care Power of Attorney. No one plans to be incapacitated, but if you are, who will make health care decisions for you? You must make sure to complete a health care power of attorney so you can be protected. In this document, you appoint a trusted individual (and an alternate) to make important medical decisions for you in the event you are unable to make them for yourself. Make sure your wishes are respected by giving a copy of your health care power of attorney to your physician.

Always designate alternates. Extend the usefulness of your estate documents by appointing more than one agent to represent your interests. In this way, if your first choice isn't available, you've already provided for one or more alternates, so a choice is not made for you.

Update your estate plan. Keep current: be sure to review your estate planning documents every three years or so to ensure they are still current. Changes in personal circumstances, economic fortunes and tax laws may warrant revisions.

Ensure protection from creditors. Safeguard your assets. If you have concerns about your creditors or your children's creditors, consider transferring your assets to a trust to limit creditor access to your assets. Trusts can be drafted with special protective provisions, providing you have not already incurred the debt.

Check your beneficiary designation forms. Wills are not the only documents that govern the disposition of your assets. Insurance policy proceeds and retirement accounts both pass in accordance with the terms of your beneficiary designation form when you die. Make sure the information on these forms is current and accurate to ensure these assets pass to the individual(s) you intend.

Protect your homestead. The best deal in asset protection today is the homestead. If you own a home as your primary residence, for a modest fee you can place protection on your home from creditors for up to $500,000 of the equity in your home. Simply contact your attorney to complete and file the necessary documents.

Ensure your bank knows the people who hold your powers of attorney. If you are incapacitated and your designated Powers of Attorney (or the Trustees for your trust) need to get access to your bank accounts or safe deposit box, the bank needs to know who those people are. The easiest way to ensure this is to have the Powers of Attorney and/or Trustees sign the signature cards in person at the bank when you add their names to the list of those who can access your safe deposit box.

These tools not only serve to preserve your assets but, if properly executed, eliminate the need for your heirs to take the expensive, time-consuming path through the courts. (As an estate planner, I identify suitability and needs, and organize each set of documents according to the client's needs.)

Challenge 6: The Stock Market Myths that Just Won't Die

Have you heard market experts say, "*This is a good time to invest in the stock market*"? Really? On average, stocks provide about 10 percent return annually, according to the experts. But, this assumption goes back to the 1800s and no longer applies in the 21st century. Today, your typical annual return from investing in the stock market is closer to 5 percent.

Is your broker being paid a commission to lose your money? How can you make money without losing money?

Here's what the broker does. When he buys shares of stocks and mutual funds, he sends your money to Wall Street. Now the market can go in three directions: up, down or stagnant. Wall Street can't control the market. But brokers don't make their money by making us money, though they would like for that to happen, because it keeps us investing with them. They make their money by *managing* our money. They make money when the market goes down, when it's flat or when it goes up. They always win. We only win in one of those three directions. They win in all three directions. Though we always hope for the best, we all too often end up with a cooked goose instead of the golden egg.

I'm proud to say that I have never lost one dollar for any of my clients. I'm not a genius; it's simply because I won't put their money where it could be lost. That isn't hard to do, either. The hard part is getting clients a decent return. We did that by using specific strategies allowing them to benefit from any gains in the market while avoiding any market loss.

What did Babe Ruth do before the Great Depression? We learn from the Babe that he had a financial planner named Christie Walsh who got him into an annuity and he did not lose one dollar when the market crashed. But, as the great philosopher Georg Friedrich Hegel once said, "The only thing we learn from history is that we learn nothing from history." Let's say we had $200,000 in the market and the market went down 50 percent. Now let's say the market comes roaring back with a 50 percent gain. Am I in good shape now? Where am I? I am at $150,000; I am still down $50,000 from the $200,000. How does that happen—minus 50 percent, plus 50 percent, and I'm still down by $50,000! How big of a return do I have to have on my $100,000 to get back to $200,000? Well, 100 percent—that's a significant return. How long will it take the market to give me a total of 100 percent return? Forever, and that's too long. I'm not willing to wait for forever.

So where do you park your money? Let's find the perfect investment. What features do you want? You don't want to lose your money. You want safety, growth, and tax deferral. Yes, no tax! That's good. How much liquidity do you want? Is 100 percent okay? I have been looking for 20 years and can't find it. How close can we get?

Let's see. What would you be willing to give up? Safety? No. Opportunity for growth? No. Do you want to pay more taxes? Preferably not. Now, if you compromise on liquidity, it means you could get the other three: safety, opportunity, and less tax liability. If you have to compromise somewhere, do it on liquidity. That makes total sense. You would have safety without paying the price for it.

How would you like to take distributions from your IRA over your life expectancy and still be guaranteed more money than you ever deposited, for any beneficiary, regardless of interest rates or market fluctuations?

Find out if your current advisor is an IRA distributions specialist. Many advisors who are not trained in the new distribution rules may unknowingly be giving the IRA owner bad advice. Poor advice can result in IRA owners and their beneficiaries losing the many advantages of the new distribution rules. Here are two examples:

1. If the beneficiaries fail to take their first distribution before December 31st of the year following the year of the owners' death, the entire account may be subject to immediate taxation.

2. If the IRA owner fails to take a required minimum distribution, he/she will pay tax on the distribution and may be subject to a 50 percent excise tax, in addition to the income tax on the failed distribution. Beneficiaries who receive inaccurate advice may wind up with rapid distribution, causing rapid taxation and the loss of a lifetime of income from an inherited IRA.

In my work, I share solutions, not products. How would you like to take your Required Minimum Distribution (RMD) and leave your principal for your beneficiaries with the oldest insurance company in the world? Beneficiaries will receive 4 percent compounded, so you could take out 4 percent and still leave money for beneficiaries. The promise is that, no matter how large the IRA, beneficiaries can take their RMDs and, still at zero growth, have the original premium for their beneficiaries. It's guaranteed to never lose a dime.

RMDs guarantee your principal at death. So take your RMD, pay taxes, spend the rest of it over the course of your life and still have your original investment/ principal to leave your heirs. Here are the advantages:

- no caps
- no participation rates
- no hidden surrender charges
- interest on RMD not forfeited
- values tracked daily
- 4 percent guaranteed minimum death benefit rider
- 6 percent income rider
- guaranteed for the life of contract
- 100 percent downside protection, full value at death

This solution works no matter what the interest rates are in the marketplace.

Has anyone ever asked you, "Are you willing to sell your winners while they're winning?" If I were to ask you that, you might say, "Kris, why would I want to do that? The idea is that you want to have winners in place. Why would I want to sell the winners?"

There's no such thing as a permanently excellent company or permanently excellent industry. Everything is cyclical. You can employ the buy-and-hold strategy for a long time and if it doesn't work out—if you haven't captured the gains by the time you know it's over—you're bound to give back some or all of the gains. It's hard to make winners win in many cases because selling the very thing responsible for the gains isn't easy. Losing, of course, has its own problems.

If you're holding without a way to capture gains, you could be in a winning mutual fund for ten years. For nine of those years you win, and the tenth year experience losses that force you to return the other nine years' worth of performance. You put up the capital. You took the risk. You were patient. You were a long term investor, yet you still may not have anything to show for it. That's difficult.

Very few individuals know where to find safety and opportunity on the same dollar at the same time. But there are ways to structure your portfolio to have safety and opportunity at the same time, on the same dollar.

You see, Americans know where to find safety. Today, they're buying government bonds with a 30-year maturity. Some recent bonds have yielded zero percent from our government, and yet people park their dollars there. I'm safe, but what's the price I've paid? Not much of a return. I can't recover my losses. I may not even be able to fight inflation. The same problem exists at the bank with CDs. My clients ask me, "Kris, if you could show me how to have the safety, maybe of a bank CD or a government Treasury bond, and yet have a little better opportunity than they're offering, that would pique my interest."

Fortunately, there are ways to do exactly this.

In the middle of this timeframe, one of the greatest economic upheavals in our country, I have not lost a single client any money. You might say, "What are you doing, earning those 3, 4, and 5 percent returns?" No. We've been doing much better than that. I've actually averaged better than 7 to 8 percent in the past five years. Now 8 percent may not sound like it's setting the world on fire, but do you know according to the "Rule of 72," I can double your money in 9 years with just an 8 percent return, and I don't have to take risks to do it? Let's see how to accomplish that.

What would performance you expect from the market—maybe not right now, but normally, what would you get out of the market on an annual basis? Ten percent?

You know, ten is the most common number I hear. But in 1990, folks told me, "Kris, if you can't get me 20 percent, I'm not interested." Things change, don't they?

Now we might be happy with a zero, because it means at least I didn't lose any of my money.

Are you at the highest point you've ever been, or are you still working your way back there? "Well, no, we're getting closer," you say. So was that really a return or was that barely a recovery? See, we fool ourselves. If I had to spend 10 more years of getting 10 percent returns, it really isn't doing me a whole lot of good if I can only make back what I lost. Then when the market turns down again, we've got some more losses.

It's hard to know what to do. You say, "Well, Kris, I don't want to sell here because I'll have to take losses.... Well, I don't want to sell here because I'm making money.... Well, I don't want to sell here because my broker says it's just a correction.... Everything goes up, comes down and corrects at some point... but then it's too late. My losses are too great. See, I never can get out of the market. It never benefits me. I can't sell on the way up, and I can't sell on the way down. I'm trapped. There's got to be a better way to make my money work for me and not feel like it holds me hostage." By using the strategies I suggest, you will have the ability to capture gains systematically, on autopilot, on a regular basis, every year. That means you will only be on the up side if the market crashes. You won't be following the market down.

"The past 25 years investors have captured only about one-third of the return of the market in diversified portfolios," Warren Buffett says. "Diversification reduces our returns."

It's true that if you could predict which investment in your portfolio was going to be the winner, you could put all the money there in advance. Since you can't know that in advance, you diversify. That means the losers pull down the performance of the winners and you get some return in the middle.

You know what drove the market up like that? When there are 78 million baby boomers out of only 300 million people in our country, and those 78 million boomers start declining in their spending habits because of their stage of life—that's bound to do something to our economy.

Did you know that 70 percent of our gross domestic product is derived from consumer spending? Gross domestic product is defined as "all sales and purchases bought and sold within the borders of the U.S." Seventy percent of those sales come from people spending to buy cars, houses, almost anything. When the boomers don't need to buy the next whatever—because they already have one, or they're worried about their finances, and they keep their pocketbooks closed—we can't recover in the same way we did before.

Additionally, the free flow of access to credit, which was unprecedented leading up to October 9, 2006, helped drive the economies to bubble levels, both in real estate and the stock market. Think of the effect of removing credit for our economy! Just suppose, for example, that mortgages were illegal. How would a family just getting started, married for a few months, with college loans to pay, ever manage to find a quarter of a million dollars to buy a house? The bubble had to burst at some point or the dream of home ownership would not become a reality for many folks. So the tightening of credit can have some positive effects. But there are some major issues to resolve before we can have sustaining growth in the markets.

This isn't just my view. These observations come from Karlen Tucker, Senior Advisory Group, who has worked closely with me to help find safe investments. There are powerful strategies available for smart investors. You can go to sleep at night without having to keep an eye open to watch Wall Street because it doesn't matter. If the market goes up, you participate. If it goes down, you're protected. You never lose your principal. Even during the Great Depression, no one lost one dollar using this strategy.

Now I have to ask you a question. If the main parachute fails, how much time does the skydiver have to pull his reserve? Not much! That's about right. (Actually, it turns out that he had the rest of his life.) So when should you make a decision about protecting your profits? Right away! In survey after survey, Americans have expressed that their number one concern is outliving their life savings. Do you want a financial plan that's absolutely safe, gives you great growth and controls your taxes? Are you willing to sacrifice a little liquidity so that you never outlive your life savings, never run out of income, and leave full value at death? Do you want a solution that works no matter what the interest rates are? And no more sending your money on the roller coaster ride! This is the benefit I give my clients—a solution that works no matter what the interest rates are, or how volatile the market.

Everyone has different financial needs, and not all investments are suitable for everyone. Don't be afraid to ask for help. While estate planning is highly personal and emotional, it also involves a lot of legal, financial and tax considerations. All of these must be put in order so you are Ready for PREtirement.

Challenge 7: Having Funds for a Secure and Comfortable Retirement

Many people think that they will be secure in their retirement. After all, even if their investments are modest, they can count on Social Security to cover their living expenses. Unfortunately, Social Security may not ever cover their needs. You cannot assume that Medicare and Social Security will be sufficient to cover your needs.

Consider the case of one of my clients. John had it all planned out. He'd work until he was 70 and his wife, a nurse, turned 62. Then he'd retire and they would become "snowbirds" traveling around the country in an RV. Those plans were upended last year, when John, then 66, found out he'd be losing his job as an accountant for a major firm in California. He faced a difficult job search. So although the financial tradeoff was wrenching—his annual income is now half what it was when he was working—he felt he had little choice but to retire.

"At my age and in this job market, I didn't even consider unemployment. I just went straight to Social Security," he said.

Until now, much of the attention in this recession has been focused on the group of older workers who will toil for more years than they expected because stock market losses have put a severe dent in their retirement nest egg. However, new research suggests that a larger group of workers ages 62 to 69 could find themselves with a thornier problem: no job, no prospect for finding another, and an earlier retirement than they, or their finances, were prepared to take.

"Those people, the risk that they're subject to is not the stock market, it's the labor market," said Phillip Levine, a professor of economics at Wellesley College and co-author of a recent paper looking at that phenomenon.

Already, there are signs some older workers are falling into that trap.

Mark Hinkle, a spokesman with the Social Security Administration, said applications for retirement benefits for the fiscal year ended Sept. 30, 2009, rose 22 percent over the 2008 fiscal year, to 2.57 million. That's much higher than the 15 percent increase that had been projected because of the increase in people hitting retirement age. Hinkle said the discrepancy can be attributed to the impact of the weak economy.

By now, you may be even more discouraged. After all, I've pointed out the various challenges that you face as you age and try to plan for your family's future.

It's true that the recent economic downturns make for an even gloomier outlook, particularly if you're one of the unlucky ones who is "upside down," having lost at least half of the equity in your home. Warren Buffett says homes will become places to live, not investments. A lot of folks have put all their money in their homes, and trying to sell in this market will not get back their investments.

Furthermore, some of the largest tax increases in history are on our doorstep. Unfortunately, many people like you who have diligently planned and saved for the future will be among those most hurt. For example, when you pass away, any money left in your IRA will be taxed at ordinary income rates. If you leave a sizable amount, in the eyes of the IRS you are "rich" in the year you die, and 40 to 50 percent of your IRA may be wiped out by taxes before your heirs ever see a dime.

These are all reasons to be proactive now. No one wants to talk about death and taxes but you need to do whatever it takes to motivate yourself to invest the time now instead of putting it off until later. Believe me, that time never comes until the unexpected happens, and then you will wish that you had planned much earlier. Remember, you can be a positive and optimistic person and still plan for the worst-case scenarios. When you do, you'll experience the peace of knowing everything is covered. I call it having an Estate of Mind.

With so many changes in the investment landscape, along with ever-changing tax laws, I have been working tirelessly to include the newest strategies from some of the top PREtirement planners in the country. (We can locate products that will shield you from future tax liability. I always invite folks for a free consultation.) You may be stuck in your old habits and not open to considering new options. I encourage you to step out of the box or take a step in faith out of the habits of investment among your friends and families.

It's no secret that you'll be able to take care of yourself and your family if you plan for your financial future today. You first have to change your mindset. Then you must seek advice from qualified experts and make a plan designed to generate assets that will allow you to retire early and worry-free.

Go to the following link to download *"Retire Early—Retire Wealthy."*
http://krismillermoneymaestro.com/retireearlyretirewealthy
For more information see:
http://ReadyForPREtirement.com

International speaker and money expert Loral Langemeier contributed the following article.

Your Relationship With Money

You may not think about your relationship with money much (or at all), but you definitely should! How you think and feel about money makes a huge difference.

Today it seems more difficult for a lot of people to keep a positive mindset about their financial prospects. Everywhere you turn you hear chatter about the economic downturn. People from all walks of life are in panic mode. More and more we hear about budgeting, cut backs, layoffs and worse. It's hard to escape the negative impact of the current times. "Things aren't improving," much of the media tells us, "but they're *not* getting worse." We're being offered a *glimmer of hope*.

True hope lies in the fact that you are unique and have a skill set and talents that could take you from where you are now to where you want to be financially. You just have to decipher how to turn your current skills into a marketable commodity.

I'm generally quoted for saying, "Christopher Columbus didn't discover America so we could all get jobs!" It's true! And, America was built—as great as it is—by entrepreneurs.

What's important to remember is that YOU and only you are ultimately in control of your future. For people that are avid wealth builders, times like these call for shifting and adjusting... not panic. It's true the economy has changed. Traditional forms of wealth building may no longer apply. It's not bad; it's just different. If you're holding your breath until things even out, it's time to take in some air, my friend.

So what now?

First of all you need to examine your relationship with money. **If you have a negative attitude about your money, it's safe to say your bank account reflects that same negativity.** Start by getting all the facts.

Where do you stand? Get the details.

Once you have everything out on the table it's time to look at where you want to be. What is the exact number? How much will it take for you to be financially independent once and for all? When you have that number, take a look at the "gap." The gap is the difference between where you are right now and where you want to be. This information will allow you to start the journey of creating financial independence in your life.

Things may be better or worse than you thought but now you know where you stand. Remember if you've made some bad choices you've got to chalk it up to "you live, you learn." Dwelling on your indiscretion will get you nowhere fast. **The only way to turn it into a positive is to learn from it.** Write it out; take a moment to figure out where you went wrong. Then decide to never make the same mistake. Most importantly, forgive yourself and move on.

I bet you didn't know Microsoft, Hewlett-Packard and Disney all started during economic downturns, as did more than half of the 30 companies that comprise the Dow Jones Industrial Average. This economy is not the *end-all and be-all* that much of the media would have you believe. It's just different, so don't make it complicated. Shift and adjust your thinking. Be open to new opportunities.

My belief is that everyone has the ability to rewrite their story—to improve their relationship with money! What's the vision for your life? Define it. **Where do you want to be in one year, three years, and five years, and so on?** If you don't name your goals and create a plan, you're relying on the "park and pray" method. You and I both know that doesn't work.

It's time to get into action. Make your future better than your past. Examine your relationship with money and improve it.

If you're in financial peril, it's time to leverage your skills and talents into income. Do you know that most of you could be getting paid for things you're probably doing for free? I know, I know. I've heard it all before. You're afraid to ask for the cash. That's your relationship with money telling you you're not worth it, but you *are* worth it!

Think about it. Learn to ask for the cash and put more money in your pocket starting today.

Ready… GO!

Loral Langemeier is the CEO/Founder of Live Out Loud and best-selling author of The Millionaire Maker 3 *book series and* Put More Cash in Your Pocket.

Responding to our biggest challenges and preparing for retirement can be a daunting task. But knowing these secrets will put you on the right track, quickly and efficiently.

Go to the following link to download *"The Top 10 Tips About Retirement."*
http://krismillermoneymaestro.com/top10tips
Learn more at http://ReadyForPREtirement.com

SECRET CODES VITAL TO SURVIVAL

Every Saturday night, Frankie Scarpetta takes his wife dancing.
Slicks back his hair, splashes on cologne; he's ready for romancing.
Puts on his blue plaid suit and his yellow polka dotted tie
She smells like sweet magnolia blossom; He's her Popeye

He sings in her ear slightly off-key as usual
And those songs are always love songs; that's so typical
She nods and smiles, pretty as a picture,
And he looks in her eyes like no one's existed before her,

People are unforgettable, whether we know them or not
Whispers from a grainy old photograph, never forgot
How to treat a woman, how to treat a man,
How we all fit into the master plan
How to make it to that final climb
How to love to the end of time…

In old love songs, and in the musty yellow pages of his grandma's scented Bible
Are secret codes, vital to survival

Frankie doesn't leave his bed at Sunny Side Hillcrest
And most days he doesn't know his kin from somebody else's
And he hears the band playin' Glenn Miller, Tommy Dorsey
And his wife's there dancin' with him; she's the only thing he sees

And he sings in her ear slightly off-key as usual
And those songs are always love songs; that's so typical
It's one of the reasons why Frankie's managed to live so long
He never let go of the feeling he got when he sang those songs

People are unforgettable, whether we know them or not
Whispers from a grainy old photograph, never forgot
How to treat a woman, how to treat a man,
How we all fit into the master plan
How to make it to that final climb
How to love to the end of time…

In the musty yellow pages of grandma's scented Bible
Are secret codes, vital to survival

> *Hidden in the heart,*
> *No time or place*
> *Can touch these codes*
> *Once they've been engraved*

People are unforgettable, whether we know them or not
Whispers from a grainy old photograph, never forgot
How to treat a woman, how to treat a man,
How we all fit in the master plan
How we all fit in the master plan
How to make it to that final climb
How to love to the end of time…

In the musty yellow pages of grandma's scented Bible
Are secret codes, vital to survival

— Kris Miller/Lisa Aschmann/Kelly Swanson

Chapter 2

RETIREMENT PLANNING— THE LIVING TRUST AND YOUR ESTATE PLANNING DECISIONS

"The best way to predict your future is to create it."
— **Peter Drucker**

When Mr. and Mrs. S. first came to see me about retirement planning, they were in their 60s. They owned a small business, and Mrs. S. was a teacher at our local high school. When they walked in for their appointment, the couple seemed to be arguing. The first thing I learned, after some initial questioning, was that throughout their 20-year marriage, they had never talked about money, either with each other or with their three kids.

This was a second marriage for the couple, and there were kids on both sides whom they wanted to inherit their individual assets, while keeping those assets available during the couple's lifetime. As we discussed their situation, the wife found out that Mr. S. had maintained a separate bank account she thought he had closed. The problem was that the husband had bought a house from his son and when the deed was drawn up, the son kept his own name on it, too. When the dad and his second wife decided to sell the house, the son would not release it, even though they had paid him off and were paying the mortgage. The son would not return phone calls, so Mr. and Mrs. S. were unable to access the money they needed for unexpected business and medical expenses.

They never learned how they could have taken responsibility for their financial situation so that they would not suffer if they were to lose their jobs, health or each other.

Take Control of the Estate Planning Process

You may be wondering how you can keep these types of problems from happening to you. In other chapters, I'll offer up many different financial tips, but for now, I want to focus on the importance of taking control of your future by having a solid estate plan. Usually, people say they don't have an estate plan because they don't have enough assets and they are too young. But these excuses aren't good ones. If you have any significant assets or have family members who rely on you for support, you need to have an estate plan.

The rest of this chapter gives you an excellent overview on the subject of estate planning. The content has been excerpted by permission of K. Gabriel Heiser, J.D, elder law and estate planning attorney and author of *How to Protect Your Family's Assets from Devastating Nursing Home Costs: Medicaid Secrets* (available at www. MedicaidSecrets.com).

Among the important estate planning decisions explained are:

- wills
- living trusts
- powers of attorney
- living wills

Much of the information in this section is complicated and may be unfamiliar to you, so don't try to finish reading this chapter in one sitting! It may become overwhelming and exhausting. Instead, work on just one of the following sections at a time:

- naming your Personal Representative and, if you have minor children, naming a Guardian
- marital concerns; children's shares
- ultimate distributions; naming a Trustee
- powers of attorney; living will

If you are married or setting up a joint trust with a partner: It would be ideal for the two of you to read through the discussions that follow together and make joint decisions.

If you are currently unmarried: Just skip over anything that involves a spouse or partner.

If this process feels overwhelming or is too complicated for you to work through on your own, plan to meet with an attorney or qualified estate planner and bring an up-to-date Estate Planning Worksheet or Financial Statement with you, filled out as much as you can. In addition, there may be tax-planning options for your will or living trust, depending on the value of your estate. Because of the technical nature of this analysis, these issues should be discussed with an attorney. However, please bear in mind that any fees quoted usually include a set amount of attorney time, so to the extent you can educate yourself and make some decisions in advance, you will be able to keep the costs to a minimum.

The Difference Between A Will and a Trust

Wills and trusts often go together in a solid estate plan, but they are not the same thing and they serve different purposes. In a will, the main things you want to do are to name a Personal Representative to administer your estate and a Guardian for Minor Children if you have any. If you have a living trust, you do not need to name a Personal Representative because the Trustee will administer your trust. But it is still a good idea to have a will, or what is called a pour-over will so that you can sweep into your Trust anything you might have forgotten to include in your schedule of Trust property. (Note: This is not a substitute for properly transferring your property into the trust since these items still could potentially end up in probate.)

*"The most effective language communication is almost
an unspoken language: the language of trust."*
— **Bert Decker,** ***You've Got to Be Believed to Be Heard***

Naming a Personal Representative

Your "Personal Representative" is the person or company appointed by the court to supervise the administration of your estate. Without a will, the court picks the representative; your wishes may never be known. Only with your will can you ensure that the person you want is put in charge of your assets.

Your Personal Representative is responsible for the following:

- getting your will approved by the local probate court
- notifying all of your likely creditors
- paying all of your outstanding debts, administration expenses, and taxes
- filing your final personal income tax return
- filing income tax returns for your estate
- filing a federal estate tax return (if necessary) and any required state death tax return
- safeguarding all of your personal property
- managing the investments of your other property
- possibly arranging for the sale of some of your assets
- dividing up your property among your beneficiaries

Many of these decisions have important legal and tax consequences. As a result, your Personal Representative will probably wish to hire an attorney and/or an accountant, and possibly a financial advisor as well, to assist him or her with these duties. Your Personal Representative will be entitled to a fee for his or her services, according to the rules in your state.

Should I choose my spouse for my Personal Representative? Many people feel comfortable naming their spouse as their first choice to serve as their Personal Representative. If your spouse is willing and able to do this job, then he or she may certainly be named.

Should I choose a child for my Personal Representative? Other good choices for your Personal Representative are mature adult children. If you have two or more children, it may be a good idea to name one of them as your Personal Representative, but there are many issues that may make this choice a difficult one. For example, there may be family dynamics that lead you to name two or more (or all) of your children; one of your children may live nearby, or be more accessible or have more time in their personal schedule to handle your estate; one or more children may have more relevant professional training that would facilitate their serving as your Personal Representative. For example, one may be a lawyer, accountant, financial advisor, etc. While this is not a requirement, it is something you should carefully consider in making your choice for Personal Representative.

Should I choose a bank or trust company? There are many independent trust companies or trust departments of banks (known as "corporate fiduciaries") with powers under state law to manage estates and trusts. Note that with a small estate, you are probably better off economically naming a family member or other individual, because of the minimum fees that a corporate fiduciary must charge. However, naming a bank or trust company may be your only option if you have no suitable relative or other individual to serve as your Personal Representative.

What are the benefits of naming a Corporate Personal Representative (i.e., a bank or trust company)?

- They have vast experience handling similar estates.
- They will be around when the time comes for them to act.
- They have deep pockets to protect your beneficiaries if anything goes wrong.
- They have contacts in the community to arrange for appraisers, accountants and attorneys, as necessary.
- They will handle your estate impartially, which hopefully will prevent family squabbles over distribution of your property.

Of course, the Corporate Personal Representative charges a fee for handling your estate, so you should find out the fees of several before choosing one.

Should I name Co-Personal Representatives? You can name a single Personal Representative, or two people to serve together as Co-Personal Representatives. If you name two people to serve as Co-Personal Representatives, they both must be approved by the probate court. Both of them will need to sign all forms, approve all distributions, sign all checks, etc. Although this may be an inconvenience for them, it does help reduce the chances for mistakes or misunderstandings. It is generally not advisable to name more than two people to serve together as Co-Personal Representatives, for the simple reason that it slows everything down and increases the difficulty in managing your estate. It is also possible to name a corporate and individual Personal Representative to serve as Co-Personal Representatives, although there will not likely be any reduction in fees. In some cases, the bank or trust company will actually increase its fees, since now it has to spend more time getting the individual Personal Representative to review and approve its decisions.

In general, if there are three or more Co-Personal Representatives, a majority vote will rule. In any event, don't forget that all of the Personal Representatives are liable to your beneficiaries if they make a mistake. It is not a job to be taken lightly!

Who will serve as your initial Personal Representative(s)?

All of these will serve together as Co-Personal Representatives. Select as many of the following as you wish:

1. ❏ My surviving spouse

2. _____

3. _____

Successor Personal Representatives: A Successor Personal Representative will replace your initial Personal Representative(s) if for any reason the initial Personal Representative(s) fails or ceases to serve. For example, the Personal Representative(s) may decline to serve, or resign, become ill, or get removed by the beneficiaries (or the court) at some point in the future.

Who will serve as your Successor Personal Representative(s)?

1. _____

2. _____

3. _____

Choose one:

❏ I am naming only one Successor Personal Representative.

❏ All Successor Personal Representatives shall serve together as Co-Personal Representatives.

❏ All Successor Personal Representatives shall serve successively, in the order named.

Choose one:

❏ I want the Successor Personal Representative(s) to begin serving **only if there are NO remaining initial Personal Representatives** who can serve.

❏ I want the Successor Personal Representative(s) to begin serving **upon the first vacancy** among the initial Personal Representatives.

Examples of how to name individual Personal Representatives:

- my father, John Nichols
- my daughter-in-law, Peggy Jones
- Robert Nunez of 111 Trousdale Lane, Smithville, TX
- Bedford O'Coyne, with offices at 123A Jonesboro Ct., Denver, CO
- my son, Roger Smith, but only if he is at least 21 years of age at the time of his appointment

Naming a Guardian for Your Minor Children

If you have one or more minor children, you will need to name a Guardian in your will. Your Guardian will make personal and financial decisions for any of your minor children, if you are no longer living or are incapacitated and can no longer take care of them. Without a will, the court could pick whomever they want, and your wishes would never be known. Although the local probate court actually appoints the Guardians, the court almost always appoints the person(s) named in the parent's will.

Factors you should consider in deciding on your Guardian(s) are:

- child-rearing skills
- similar or compatible religious beliefs
- whether there are other children in their household of similar age to your children

- integrity and stability
- physical ability to care for your children
- a job situation that allows them sufficient time for your children
- financial lifestyle and philosophy
- geographical location: must your children move and leave their friends

Note that you may decide to name someone other than your Guardian to manage and invest your child's assets (i.e., in a trust for your child), so the Guardian does not necessarily need to have great money management skills.

Enter the names of the individual(s) you would like to be your Guardian(s) in the order in which you would like them to serve. If a couple is named, then both must be unable to serve as Guardian before the persons(s) in the next box will substitute for them. If you do not wish to name Successor Guardians, simply leave the lines for the second and third individuals blank.

1st individual or couple _____

2nd individual or couple _____

3rd individual or couple _____

If you are married, do not enter your spouse's name above since your Guardian(s) will only serve if your spouse does not survive you or for any other reason cannot act as parent.

Examples of how to name Guardians:

- my parents, Lois and Jim Jones
- my brother, James Smith, and his wife, Mary Smith
- Robert Nunez of 111 Trousdale Lane, Smithville, TX
- Bedford O'Coyne, with offices at 123A Jonesboro Ct., Denver, CO
- my son, Roger Smith, but only if he is at least 21 years of age at the time of his appointment

> *"To be prepared is half the victory."*
> **— Miguel de Cervantes**

Specific Distributions

This section deals with distributions of cash or specific property, to be made before any other distributions under your will. If you have a living trust, you can make these specific distributions in the trust instead. Most people like to rely on a handwritten memorandum that may be changed at any time, without a trip in to see the attorney every time a change is made. If that is agreeable to you, then you may skip this section. However, if you plan to leave cash to certain individuals or institutions or you really want to make sure a gift of personal property is put in the body of your will (or living trust), then indicate that here:

Marital Concerns

Husband/Partner 1: please check any one or more of the following that is true:

- ☐ My wife/partner is not a good money manager.
- ☐ I'm concerned that my wife/partner may be taken advantage of after my death and "talked out of" her or his life savings or sold inappropriate investments.
- ☐ I'd like to ensure that what I leave my wife/partner will pass to my children after her/his death.
- ☐ I'm concerned that my wife/partner may remarry and that the new spouse/partner may wind up with my assets after my wife/partner's death or divorce, and I want to make sure my children are protected.
- ☐ Regardless of the above issues, I prefer to give my wife/partner as much control over my share of our property as possible.

Wife/Partner 2: please check any one or more of the following that is true:

- ☐ My husband/partner is not a good money manager.
- ☐ I'm concerned that my husband/partner may be taken advantage of after my death and "talked out of" his/her life savings or sold inappropriate investments.
- ☐ I'd like to ensure that what I leave my husband/partner will pass to my children after his/her death.
- ☐ I'm concerned that my husband/partner may remarry and that the new spouse/partner may wind up with my assets after my husband/partner's death or divorce, and I want to make sure my children are protected.
- ☐ Regardless of the above issues, I prefer to give my husband/partner as much control over my share of our property as possible.

If you indicated that you are concerned that your property may not ultimately pass to your children if your spouse/partner remarries, your will (or living trust) can state that if your spouse/partner remarries after your death, distributions to your spouse/partner from your estate will be limited unless your spouse/partner has signed a premarital ("prenuptial") agreement with the new spouse/partner, stating that each spouse/partner is free to dispose of his or her own assets in the event of a divorce and following death.

☐ Yes, we would each like to have this included in our will (or living trust).

☐ We're not sure; we would like to discuss this in more detail with you at our meeting.

Children's Shares—
Creation of Trust for Minor and/or Adult Children

Although most people's initial inclination is to leave an adult child's share to the child outright, there are many advantages to holding a child's share in a trust.

The basic benefits are:

- The trust assets are invested and distributed by a Trustee, and therefore protected from the child's mismanagement.
- Creditors of the child are prevented from attaching the trust assets. If the child is sued for any reason, the trust assets are protected.
- If the child is ever divorced, the spouse is prevented from reaching the trust assets. With the divorce rate approaching 50 percent, this must be considered a realistic possibility.
- The trust assets are not taxed in the child's own estate. This could save many thousands of dollars in estate taxes at the child's death.

These benefits apply regardless of the age of the child and even if your child serves as Trustee. If you are concerned that the child may resent having his or her share "tied up in trust," you should consider allowing the child to serve as the sole Trustee of the child's own trust upon attaining a certain age. (You will be able to select this option later in the process.) Once the child realizes he or she has complete control over the trust investments and distributions, and that the assets are protected against creditors, divorces, and estate taxes, the child will be glad you had the foresight to set up such a trust!

After you have finished reading the above discussion about a child's trust, choose one of the following:

☐ I would like to leave a child's share to the child outright, free of trust. (If you check this box, you can skip down to "Ultimate Distributions," below.)

☐ I would like to leave a child's share in a trust for the child's benefit. I will choose the terms of the trust in the next few sections.

The Common Trust

What is a common trust? If you have two or more children and at least one child is under age 25 or so, you may prefer to hold all of the assets in one, single trust until the youngest child attains, say, age 25. This trust (called a "common trust") will allow the education expenses of younger children to be paid before you divide your property into separate shares for each child. After all, what if you had paid the college expenses of an older child and then died? If your will (or living trust) immediately divides your property into separate shares for each child, then the child who has not yet been to college is at a disadvantage, since that child will have to pay for his or her college expenses out of his or her own share. Using a common trust gives each child the opportunity to have his or her college expenses paid before your property is divided into separate shares for the children.

The common trust will permit distributions for all of your children, for their health, education, maintenance and support, in the Trustee's discretion. Thus, even though a separate share may not be created for a child, he or she may still receive distributions from the trust, if the Trustee determines there's a need to do so. The main difference is that a distribution to one child is charged against the common trust as a whole, not just against the share of the child for whom the distribution is made.

If your children are far apart in age, you may decide not to do this, since it forces the older child(ren) to wait for many more years before they receive their separate property.

If your estate is large enough, it is simpler immediately to divide into separate shares, since the college expenses will not be an undue burden on a younger child. This is a judgment call, since it depends on the value of your assets at the time your property will be distributed to your children, the likelihood your children will attend college, and the cost of the college at that time. In general, the older your children are at the time you make your will (or living trust), the less likely you will need a common trust for your children.

After you have finished considering whether you want to establish a common trust, choose one of the following:

❐   I would like to leave my children's shares in a common trust for the benefit of all my children. End the common trust when the youngest child attains age (select one):

    ❐   21   ❐   25   ❐____.

❏ I do not want a common trust in my will (or living trust) and instead wish to divide my property into shares for my children immediately upon my death (or, if married, upon the death of the spousal survivor.).

Terms of the Child's Trust

There are basically three options for a child's trust, which are explained below:

- hold a child's share in trust for the lifetime of the child
- make several staggered distributions to the child over a period of time
- hold a child's share in trust until a certain age

Lifetime Trust. This is recommended for the larger estates, if a child's share will be over $300,000. It protects the child's share from divorce, lawsuits, and creditors of the child, and excludes the property from the child's taxable estate. Assuming you name the child as his or her own Trustee, the child will have a great deal of control over the property yet still have all of these protections.

Staggered Distributions. If you are uncomfortable with the idea of a lifetime trust, or there simply are not enough assets to make that worthwhile, consider a trust with discretionary distributions. Under this type, distributions of one-third of the trust are made outright to the child at a stated age, half the balance five years later, and the full balance five years after that. This is a compromise solution.

All in Trust Until a Certain Age: If the child's share is even a smaller amount, this option may be best. It holds the child's share in a trust, protecting the assets from squandering and mismanagement by the child, and when the child reaches a stated age, the assets are simply distributed to the child outright, free of trust.

After you have understood the options for a child's trust, choose one of the following:

❏ I would like to hold a child's share in trust for the child for the child's lifetime. During the child's lifetime, the Trustee may make distributions to the child for the child's health, education, maintenance and support.

❏ I would also like the Trustee to have the discretion to make distributions to the child's own descendants as well as to the child.

Why this is recommended: Allowing the Trustee to make distributions to the child's own children increases the usefulness of the trust. Since the trust will last for the lifetime of your child, your child may wish to use the trust assets to pay for the child's own children's expenses, such as college, or starting a business or profession. If the child had to pay for these expenses directly, the child could be making taxable gifts when he or she makes those payments or distributions to his or her own children. If the Trustee of the child's trust makes these distributions, however, the distributions are not subject to gift taxes.

☐   I would like to make staggered distributions to the child, as follows:

- One-third to the child upon the child attaining at least age ___. (Enter a number for the age of the first distribution to your child. Most people consider age 21 to be a minimum age, but 25 or even 30 are also common ages for the first distribution to a child.) If the child has already reached that age at the time the trust is created (but is not yet five years older than that age), then the child will receive one-third of the trust assets at that time.
- One-half the balance of the trust when the child is five years older than the age entered above. If the child has already reached that age at the time the trust is created, then the child will receive one-half of the trust assets at that time.
- The full balance of the trust when the child is 10 years older than the age entered above. If the child has already reached that age at the time the trust is created, then the child will receive the entire trust share, outright.

Prior to each age, the Trustee may make distributions to the child for the child's health, education, maintenance and support, out of trust income or principal.

☐   I would like to hold a child's share in trust until the child attains at least age ___. Prior to that age, the Trustee may make distributions to the child for the child's health, education, maintenance and support.

"Special Needs Trust" for a Disabled Child

If you have a child who is disabled or has "special needs," you should consider holding that child's share of your estate in a specially designed trust for the lifetime of the child. The terms of this "special needs trust" will be set forth in your will (or living trust), and it will state that the trust assets may only be used to supplement and not replace any benefits that are otherwise available to your child from any governmental source, such as SSI, Medicaid or Social Security.

This will allow your child's share of your estate to be used to pay for expenses that are not provided for by the government, such as clothing, a TV, a computer, certain medical treatments they refuse to pay for, etc. In addition, there are certain programs for disabled children that are only available through the government, if the child qualifies. Use of the special needs trust will help ensure that such benefits and programs will be available for your child.

☐ Yes, please hold my child's share in a special needs trust. Enter full legal name of child for whom the special needs trust will be created:

_____

☐ No, do not set up a special needs trust for my child.
☐ I'm not sure; I would like to discuss this in more detail with you at our meeting.

Ultimate Distributions

If, before all of your property is distributed, all of the people named in your will (or living trust) are deceased—including your spouse and all of your descendants—to whom would you like the assets to pass? Since this may occur upon the termination of a trust you have created for someone else, within your will or living trust, it may be many years after your own death.

☐ 100 percent to my heirs under state law (please check law for your state).

Your "heirs" are those individuals who would receive your property if you died without a will. Which relatives get how much of your estate depends upon the state law in effect at the time of your death. For example, currently under Colorado law, if your parents are living when you pass away, your estate property would go to each of them in equal shares or all to the survivor of the couple. If your parents are no longer living, your estate property would go equally to your siblings, with the share of the deceased sibling passing to that sibling's descendants. If none of those people are then living, your property would pass to your more remote relatives, in the percentages set forth under state law. (Again, you'll need to check your particular state laws.)

If you are married, especially if it is a second marriage for one or both spouses/partners and there are children from previous marriages, consider choosing the following option instead of the one above (most common):

❐ 50 percent to my heirs and 50 percent to my partner's heirs.

Why choose 50/50 to heirs of both partners? You generally will not know which partner will die first. In most cases, the assets of both spouses will wind up being owned by the surviving spouse. Therefore, if each will (or living trust) states "Leave the property to my heirs only," then one side of the family or the other side will wind up with all of the assets of both partners, based solely on the chance occurrence of who dies second, even if the deaths are only a short time apart. Therefore, most couples feel that it is fairer to divide the assets between the heirs on both partners' sides of the family.

Occasionally, if one partner has most of the assets, the partners agree that the heirs on that partner's side of the family should inherit the remaining assets under this section. It is a good idea to discuss this issue with your partner so you both have compatible wills (or living trusts).

Consider making a gift to one or more religious or charitable organizations you want to support:

❐ To the following individuals and/or religious or charitable organizations:
   • in equal shares, or
   • in the percentages indicated

Estate planning is not just for people who are old or have lots of money. Estate planning is for everyone.

Go to the following link to download, *"Estate Planning Is For Everyone."*
http://krismillermoneymaestro.com/estate-planning-is-for-everyone
Learn more at http://ReadyForPREtirement.com.

"Be careful the environment you choose for it will shape you;
be careful the friends you choose for you will become like them."
— W. Clement Stone

Naming a Trustee

Review this next section only if:

- your will is going to contain a trust for your spouse or children, or
- you are creating a living trust

Your "Trustee" is the person or company named in your will (or living trust), to manage, invest, and distribute the assets held in the trust(s) created inside your will (or living trust).

What Does a Trustee Do? Your Trustee is responsible for the following:

- managing the investment of the trust property
- filing income tax returns for the trust
- preparing an annual account of trust investments and distributions
- arranging for the sale of some of the trust assets, from time to time
- deciding whether to make a distribution to your beneficiaries and the amount of such distributions at the termination of a trust; dividing up the property among your beneficiaries

Many of these decisions have important legal and tax consequences. As a result, your Trustee will probably wish to hire an attorney and/or an accountant, and possibly a financial advisor as well, to assist him or her with these duties. Your Trustee will be entitled to a fee for his or her services, as provided in your will.

Whom Should I Name as My Trustee? If you are creating your own living trust, most people prefer serving as a Trustee of their own living trust. This especially makes sense if you are currently managing your own investments (with or without professional help). Most married couples name both spouses as Co-Trustees of their living trust which gives both spouses immediate access to the trust assets should one of them become disabled or die.

If you are creating a will that contains a trust, you can't name yourself as Trustee of a trust under your own will, since you won't be living at that time! It is common to use the same parties you named as your Personal Representatives also to serve as your Trustees, who may also be beneficiaries under the will or trust. Most people feel comfortable naming their partner as their first choice to serve as Trustee under their will. If your partner is willing and able to do this job, then he or she may certainly be named as Trustee.

Naming a Child as Trustee. Other good choices for your Trustee are mature, adult children. If you have two or more children, it may be a good idea just to name one of them as your Trustee, but there are many issues that make this choice either an easy or a difficult one. For example, there may be family dynamics that lead you to name two or more (or all) of your children; one of your children may live nearby, or be more accessible or have more time in their personal schedule to handle the management of the trust; one or more children may have more relevant professional training, such as in law, finance, or accounting, that would facilitate their serving as your Trustee. While these skills and training are not a requirement to be a Trustee, you should carefully consider a person's background in making your choice for Trustee.

Naming a Bank or Trust Company: If for any reason you do not wish to name your spouse or children you may wish to name a different relative, other suitable individual, or a corporate fiduciary to serve as your Trustee. A "corporate fiduciary" is an independent trust company or the trust department of a bank, with powers under state law to manage estates and trusts. They may be your only option if you have no suitable relative or other individual to serve as your Trustee.

What are the benefits of naming corporate Trustees?

- They have vast experience handling similar trusts.
- They will be around when the time comes for them to act.
- They have deep pockets to protect your beneficiaries if anything goes wrong.
- They have contacts in the community to arrange for appraisals, accountants and attorneys, as necessary.
- They will handle all trust distributions impartially, which hopefully will prevent family squabbles.

Of course, the corporate Trustee charges a fee for its services, so you should ask around to find out their fees before naming them.

Naming Co-Trustees. You can name a single Trustee or two people to serve together, as Co-Trustees. Both of them will need to sign all forms, approve all distributions, sign all checks, etc. Although this may be an inconvenience for them, it does help reduce the chances for mistakes or misunderstandings.

It is not advisable to name more than two people to serve together as Co-Trustees, for the simple reason that it slows everything down and increases the difficulty in managing your estate. In general, if there are three or more Co-Trustees, a majority vote will rule. In any event, don't forget that all of the Trustees are liable to your beneficiaries if they make a mistake. It is not a job to be taken lightly!

Examples of how to name individual Trustees:

- my father, John Nichols
- my daughter-in-law, Peggy Jones
- Robert Nunez of 111 Trousdale Lane, Smithville, TX
- Bedford O'Coyne, with offices at 123A Jonesboro Ct., Denver, CO
- my son, Roger Smith, but only if he is at least 21 years of age at the time of his appointment
- AmSouth Bank, with its main office in Nashville, TN

Initial Trustees

If you are making a will with a trust in it, and not a living trust, answer the following questions:

Based on the information above, whom would you like to name as the initial Trustee(s) of the trust(s) under your will? (Select as many of the following as you wish. All of these will serve together as your initial Trustees.)

- ☐ I wish to use the same individual(s) and/or trust company as I named for my Personal Representative(s). **(If you check this box, *you are done!* Congratulations!)**
- ☐ I wish to use *different* parties for my Trustee(s) than the one(s) I named for my Personal Representative(s). Here are my choices:

Who will serve as your *initial* Trustee(s)? (All of these will serve together as Co-Trustee[s].) Select as many of the following as you wish.

- ☐ My surviving spouse/partner (if any)
- ☐ An individual _____

❑ Another individual _____

❑ A corporate Trustee _____

If you are making a living trust, answer the following question:

Based on the information above, whom would you like to name as the initial Trustee(s) of your living trust? (Select as many of the following as you wish. All of these will serve together as your initial Trustees.)

❑ Me

❑ My spouse/partner

❑ An individual _____

❑ Another individual _____

❑ A corporate Trustee _____

Successor Trustees

Answer this section if you are making a will with a trust in it or a living trust.

Successor Trustees: A Successor Trustee will replace your initial Trustee(s) if for any reason the initial Trustee(s) fails or ceases to serve. For example, the Trustee(s) may decline to serve, or resign, become ill, or get removed by the beneficiaries (or the court) at some point in the future.

Who will serve as your Successor Trustee(s)?

1. _____

2. _____

3. _____

Choose one:

❑ I am naming only one Successor Trustee, above.

❑ All Successor Trustees shall serve together as Co-Trustees

❑ All Successor Trustees shall serve successively, in the order named.

Choose one:

❑ I want the Successor Trustee(s) to begin serving **only if there are NO remaining initial Trustees** who can serve.

❑ I want the Successor Trustee(s) to begin serving **upon the first vacancy** among the initial Trustees.

"Nobody cares how much you know,
until they know how much you care."
— **Theodore Roosevelt**

Powers of Attorney

A "power of attorney" is a document where you give someone (called your "Agent") the legal authority to make decisions for you and carry out your wishes. This would typically apply if you became incapacitated and therefore unable to make these decisions yourself.

In most states, there are two kinds of powers of attorney: one for financial and legal decisions, and one for health and medical decisions.

Your Financial Durable Power of Attorney: The Agent under your financial durable power of attorney will be authorized to make all decisions related to your assets on your behalf, even if you become incapacitated. Your Agent will be able to do any of the following: pay your bills; sign your name on checks, deeds, contracts, and income tax returns; buy, sell, lease, mortgage any real estate; buy insurance, make loans, hire attorneys or accountants, etc.

Spouse/Partner as Agent: Many people feel comfortable naming their spouse/ partner as their first choice to serve as their Agent. If your spouse/partner is willing and able to do this job, then he or she may certainly be named.

Child as Agent: Other good choices for your Agents are stable, adult children. If you have two or more children, it may be more efficient to name just one of them as your Agent, but, as with naming a Trustee discussed above, there are many issues that can make this choice an easy or a difficult one. Factors such as family dynamics, proximity, flexibility of schedule, and relevant professional training can influence your choice of Agent.

Choosing More than One Agent: Naming more than one Agent to serve at a time will require all of them to (1) be available for all financial decisions, and (2) agree on all decisions. If efficiency were the only concern, it is better to name just one individual as your Primary Agent and have one or more Successor Agents to serve, successively, as backups. However, you may prefer that all of your children have to get together and make these important decisions, if you are incapacitated.

If you are unsure about whom or how many people to name as your Agent, consider speaking with your spouse/partner, children, attorney or other trusted advisor for additional input.

Examples of how to name individual Agents:

- my father, John Nichols
- my daughter-in-law, Peggy Jones
- Robert Nunez of 111 Trousdale Lane, Smithville, TX
- Bedford O'Coyne, with offices at 123A Jonesboro Ct., Denver, CO
- my son, Roger Smith, but only if he is at least 21 years of age at the time of his appointment

Who would you like to name as your "Agent" to make financial and legal decisions for you, if you became incapacitated? All of these will serve together as your initial Agent(s).

- ❏ My spouse/partner _____
- ❏ An individua _____
- ❏ Another individual _____

Please name at least one Successor Agent:

- ❏ An individual _____
- ❏ Another individual _____
- ❏ Another individual _____

Please select one of the following options:

- ❏ All Successor Agents shall serve together as Co-Agents.
- ❏ All Successor Agents shall serve successively, in the order named.

Agents Acting Independently: If you have two or more Co-Agents and wish for any one of them to have the power to make financial decisions for you, then permit them to act independently. This would be useful where one Agent lives near you but the other lives far away, or travels a lot, etc. Of course, this also permits them to give conflicting directions to financial institutions, so it should be considered carefully. The alternative is to require all Co-Agents to participate in every financial decision. This is less efficient, but it does result in a unified decision being presented at all times.

May the Agents act independently (as opposed to jointly), on all decisions? (If three or more to serve together, it will be by majority vote.)

☐ Yes, I wish to allow each Agent to act independently of the others.
☐ No, I wish to require all Agents to decide together on all decisions.

When Should the Power of Attorney Become Effective?

If your power of attorney becomes effective immediately, it will be easier for your Agents to utilize the document should an emergency arise. On the other hand, it is also possible that this could more easily lead to abuse by your Agent. (However, if you have any doubts about the honesty of your named Agent, this would indicate that you should not name this individual as your Agent in the first place!)

If your power of attorney only becomes effective upon your incapacity, your Agents would have to obtain a doctor's certification that you were incapacitated before your Agents would have any power under your document.

Your selection depends on how well you know the individuals you have chosen to be your Agents.

When shall your power of attorney become effective?

☐ Immediately upon signing
☐ Only upon my incapacity

Your Health Care Power of Attorney: who would you like to name as your Agent to make medical and health care decisions for you, if you became incapacitated?

☐ The same parties I chose for my financial durable power of attorney (most common)
Otherwise, indicate your choices below for initial and successor Agents.

All of these will serve together as my initial Agent(s):

☐ My spouse/partner
☐ An individual _____
☐ Another individual _____

Please name at least one Successor Agent:

- ☐ An individual _____ _
- ☐ Another individual _____
- ☐ Another individual _____

Please select one of the following options:

- ☐ All Successor Agents shall serve together as Co-Agents.
- ☐ All Successor Agents shall serve successively, in the order named.

Agents Acting Independently: may the Agents act independently (as opposed to jointly) on all decisions? (If three or more to serve together, it will be by majority vote.)

- ☐ Yes, I wish to allow each Agent to act independently of the others.
- ☐ No, I wish to require all Agents to decide together on all decisions.

Your Living Will

Your living will is a document that states your wishes regarding the extent of medical intervention to prolong your life, or not, under certain circumstances. For example, in your living will, you can direct that you not be kept alive on tubes, machines, etc., if you have a terminal medical condition with no hope of survival. In other words, if you are dying and not expected to live very long, you may direct that you be allowed to die, regardless of what the doctors or hospital may do to artificially prolong the functioning of your physical body.

This is particularly important since modern technology has made it possible to artificially prolong life beyond natural limits and the bias in hospitals is often towards doing anything and everything to prolong life, regardless of the quality—or lack thereof—of life. This extension of life may result in a loss of dignity and cause unnecessary pain and suffering while providing nothing other than artificial support of bare functions for the patient.

This does NOT mean that if you are otherwise healthy, but have a heart attack, the hospital will simply let you die. However, if you are dying from, for example, cancer, and are at the end of your ability to fight off this disease, your living will will permit you to die a natural death with only the administration of pain relief medication. If you do not have a living will, then your physicians may be unable to end such artificial life support, regardless of what your family tells them.

Artificially Provided Food and Water

In some states, you must make a separate decision about whether you authorize the withholding or withdrawal of food and water. This only covers the situation where you are unable to feed yourself and are dying from a terminal illness.

Do you wish to specifically authorize the withholding or withdrawal of artificially provided food, water or other nourishment or fluids? Please check one of the following two options:

❏ Yes
❏ No

Organ Donation

Please check the appropriate box below regarding your wishes to donate or not donate your organs and/or tissues for transplantation, or any of them as specifically indicated below.

If you choose to donate one or more organs or tissues, your attending physician, following your death, will be permitted to maintain you on artificial support systems only for the period of time required to maintain the viability of and to remove such organs and/or tissues.

❏ I desire to donate my organs and/or tissues for transplantation.
❏ I desire to donate ONLY the following specific organs and/or tissues for transplantation:

_____

_____

_____

❏ I DO NOT desire to donate any of my organs or tissues for transplantation.

Time for Changes: PREpare for PREtirement

From Family Organizer *by Dr. Brian Kluth and used by permission.*

When should you consider changing or updating your existing will, trust, living will, estate, or charitable giving plans? Whenever...

- You need to change your estate executor, Personal Representative, Power of Attorney, or medical Power of Attorney because you have changed your mind, the person has died, or the selected person cannot fulfill this role.
- Additional children have been born or adopted, or your choice(s) of Guardians for underage children has changed.
- You want to restate your end-of-life medical preferences and wishes.
- You have moved to a different state or have purchased real estate in a different state.
- Your financial affairs and assets have changed.
- You desire to make a specific or significant charitable gift to a church, ministry, or nonprofit organization.
- A beneficiary has died.
- Tax laws have changed that will impact your estate.
- Professional advisors have shown you ways to restructure your estate plans to decrease your tax liability and increase the amount you can leave to children, church, Christian ministries, or charities.
- Your attorney, accountant, or estate planner has advised you that changes are necessary.
- Your spouse/partner has died, or you have become divorced.
- You want to include additional individuals in your estate plans (i.e., new grandchildren or great-grandchildren).
- You want to change (add, delete, modify) how much a specific individual, church, ministry, or charity receives.

"There are only two ways to live your life. One is as though nothing is a miracle. The other is as though everything is."
— **Albert Einstein**

Everyone dreams of a happy retirement, free from the worries of everyday working life. But is a happy retirement just a dream? Not if you make the right preparations early.

Go to the following link to download *"Happy Retirement."*
http://krismillermoneymaestro.com/happyretirment
For more information see: http://ReadyForPREtirement.com.

Estate Planning Tools for Charitable Giving

Used with permission from Family Organizer *by Dr. Brian Kluth of www. myfamilyforms.com, adapted from materials by Dick Edic of www.visionresourcing.com.*

Author's note: Even though the below article concentrates on Christian organizations, organizations of any religion or charity can benefit from these estate planning tools.

In 2 Kings 20:1, the prophet Isaiah said to King Hezekiah, "Put your house in order, because you are going to die; you will not recover." God was telling Hezekiah to complete his estate planning, so that when he died, his wishes could be carried out by those who survived him. Proverbs 13:22 says, "A good man leaves an inheritance for his children's children."

Many people feel strongly that the gifts of money and other resources accumulated through hard work and the grace of helpful circumstances, good fortune, and the right timing should be shared with others and should be used to build a better world for all. On a practical level, estate planning involves creating the right legal documents that will direct the process of settling your estate and transfer your property efficiently while minimizing probate and tax expense. Yet, in a broader sense, estate planning is the process of articulating and taking a stand for your values and priorities. Estate planning provides you with an opportunity to order your affairs in such a way that after you die, your assets can positively affect the people in your life. The estate plan itself guides those who will assist you in achieving your estate planning goals, which may include a charitable legacy. The estate planning process is the opportunity to leave charitable gifts, gifts that will continue the work and promote the values that you have held dear and worked towards fulfilling during your lifetime.

Here is a list of helpful tools for giving gifts from your current assets or estate plans.

Bequests: A bequest through a will or trust is the most common type of planned gift. Almost every adult should have a will or living trust, and every Christian or religious person should at least consider making gifts to their church, synagogue, temple, mosque or favorite charities through his or her estate. According to one set of beliefs, everything a person owns (during life and at death) belongs to God, and a person should distribute these possessions to family members, friends, and ministries that will use those assets in a way that honors all living beings. A gift through a will or trust can be a specified dollar amount or a percentage of the estate. Since the final size of the estate is uncertain at the time the will is written, it is often more desirable to use percentages than dollar amounts to describe how the estate is to be distributed. One of the benefits of a will or trust is that it can be changed at any time. A person can reevaluate his or her giving priorities as family and financial circumstances change over time. Any gift through a will or trust to a qualified charity is deductible for federal estate tax purposes.

Life Estate Gift: You may deed a personal residence, farm, or other real property through your will or trust to a nonprofit organization or religious institution to do good works in the world, like feeding the hungry, housing the homeless, building communities, protecting the environment, and at the same time, retain lifetime enjoyment and use of the property. You may continue to live in the home and, in the case of other property, you may continue to collect any income generated. You would continue to pay the taxes, insurance, and maintenance of the property and enjoy all the benefits of ownership. Upon your death, the property becomes the immediate property of the beneficiary, that is, the nonprofit organization or religious institution whom you name in your will or trust. If desired, the beneficiary may sell the property and use the cash proceeds. In the case of a personal residence left to a church or ministry, for example, the church or ministry may decide to keep the home for use by pastoral staff or visiting missionaries, or for ministry expansion.

An irrevocable Life Estate Gift such as this will generate a tax-deductible gift based on the "remainder interest" the person holds in the property. This value is determined according to government tables and the person's age. This amount may be claimed as a deduction for federal income tax purposes in the year the irrevocable Life Estate Gift is completed. This arrangement removes the gift property from the estate, and it will not be subject to either probate or the federal estate tax.

Life Insurance Gifts: Life insurance is one way of making a larger gift than a person may be able to make otherwise. This gift option is available for both new and existing policies. If done properly, the annual premiums paid on the policy can be deducted as a charitable gift for federal income tax purposes. Generally, life insurance proceeds are included in the gross estate for calculation of the federal estate tax. However, if the beneficiary of the policy is a qualified charity, there is a charitable deduction for purposes of the federal estate tax.

Life Insurance Gifts are made for a number of reasons and in a number of ways. Sometimes people have old life insurance policies they no longer need. They may be paid-up policies with significant cash value. These policies can be gifted directly to a nonprofit organization or religious institution, which, in turn can decide whether to cash out the policies or wait to receive the death benefits. Another option is to encourage people to add their church or a ministry as one of the beneficiaries of an existing policy. Some people also choose to use the concept of "tithing" their life insurance proceeds just like in their will or living trust. They do this by changing their beneficiary designations.

Charitable Remainder Unitrust: Sometimes called a "CRUT," it is designed for the person who wants to make a gift to a nonprofit organization or religious institution, but needs income during his or her lifetime. This trust is especially suited for a person with highly appreciated property (either securities or real estate). It is possible to transfer the property to the trust and avoid all tax on capital gain. A federal income tax deduction is available for the year the trust is created. It is based on the value of the trust, the age of the person, and the payout percentage selected.

A Charitable Remainder Unitrust may be created and funded at the time of death for the benefit of one or more survivors. Assets transferred to the trust would not be subject to probate or the federal estate tax. One or more charitable beneficiaries may be named in the trust. At the death of the person, the assets from the trust would be distributed to these charities. The Charitable Remainder Unitrust is one of the most technical gift plans, and requires expert help to both set up and manage. The denominational foundation or independent counsel of the religious institution or nonprofit organization you have chosen as a beneficiary should be able to assist you to set up a Charitable Remainder Unitrust from the beginning to the end of this process.

Charitable Lead Trust: This is almost the opposite of the Charitable Remainder Unitrust. The person creates a trust to provide current income to a charitable organization for a specified period of time (5, 10, 15, or more years). At the end of that time the assets of the trust are returned to family members. The Charitable Lead Trust may help wealthy families transfer assets to heirs, with little or no estate or gift tax. Since this type of trust also requires expert help to both set up and manage, seek professional counsel.

Gift Annuity Agreement/Deferred Gift Annuity Agreement: This is a perfect plan for a person who wants to make a future gift and receive a guaranteed stream of income for life. Annuity rates are based on age, and often are quite competitive with what a person can earn from low risk investments in the market. A deferred payment annuity allows for payments to begin at a later date (such as at retirement), and results in both a larger charitable gift and a greater annual income. Both immediate and deferred annuity plans are an excellent means of "supplementing" retirement income, but are not meant to be retirement plans.

Charitable Gift Annuity: This is less complicated than the Charitable Remainder Unitrust described above, but the CRUT has greater flexibility and applications. This plan provides a federal income tax deduction in the year that the annuity is entered. The amount of the gift is determined by the age of the annuitant, the annuity rate, and the principal amount. Another advantage of the gift annuity is that part of the annual income is considered tax-exempt. Also, if the annuity is funded with appreciated securities, there is significant savings related to capital gains tax. A portion of the capital gain is avoided altogether, and the remainder is reported in small increments over the life expectancy of the annuitant. All remaining funds in the agreement at the annuitant's death are available for the religious institution or nonprofit organization designated by the person. The amount placed in the annuity during life is removed from the estate and will not be subject to probate or the federal estate tax. NOTE: The Gift Annuity Agreement and Deferred Gift Annuity Agreement are less complicated than the Charitable Remainder Trust. However, few religious institutions and nonprofit organizations would be able to administer their own annuity program. Again, refer to your denominational or independent counsel, or get help from the National Christian Community Foundation (www.nationalchristian.com, 800-681-6223) in Atlanta, GA, which can provide planned giving administration services.

Living Trust: A living trust is a good "will substitute" estate planning tool for some families. Such a trust can be written to include a charitable bequest, just like in a will. Assets in the trust are distributed according to the terms of the trust and do not pass through the probate process.

> *"The purpose of life is to discover your gift.*
> *The meaning of life is to give your gift away."*
> **— David Viscott**

Naming a religious institution or nonprofit organization as a beneficiary: One easy method of making a planned gift is by naming the religious institution or nonprofit organization as beneficiary of any account that allows such a designation. A checking account or savings account would be one example. In a banking situation, this is often known as a Pay on Death (or POD) account. Some institutions may refer to this arrangement as Transfer on Death (or TOD). These arrangements allow for the assets to pass directly to the named beneficiary and avoid the probate process.

Retirement Plans: These allow the owner to name a beneficiary, or beneficiaries. At the death of some high wealth individuals, there may be two taxes levied against a qualified or tax-deferred retirement account: income and estate. These taxes can be avoided if the "secondary" beneficiary of the plan is a qualified charity. This is "win-win" because family members would end up inheriting the same amount or more when using this tax strategy. But the amount that would have been paid in tax is instead donated to the religious institution or nonprofit organization to continue their good works. With married couples, when a spouse dies, the "primary" beneficiary is usually the other spouse. The surviving spouse could then "roll" the tax-deferred retirement account into a personal tax-deferred retirement account and continue to defer any income taxes. And when he or she dies and the proceeds of the account go to a "non-spouse," like children, that becomes a "taxable event." Current tax laws allow children to "stretch out" their receipt and subsequent taxation of the proceeds. However, by naming a church, ministry, or charity as the "secondary" beneficiary, some or all of potential income taxes can be avoided. Since other assets in the estate may not be subject to income taxes at death, such as cash, life insurance or real estate, consider "using" the tax-deferred retirement account for any charitable gifts and pass the other assets to children or friends.

Automatic Transfers at death are often referred to as "will substitute" because they bypass distribution through the will. Such transfers avoid the probate process. These assets will avoid the federal estate tax when transferred to a qualified charity. Examples are joint tenancy, life insurance, IRAs and business agreements.

> *"If you want to lift yourself, lift up someone else."*
> — **Booker T. Washington**

Endowment or Scholarship Funds can be set up so that members can make current or deferred gifts into the endowment or scholarship fund knowing that it will annually give from the earnings of the investment portfolio in the fund. These funds can produce an economic "hedge" against hard times.

Outright Gifts (other than cash): Gifts other than cash can be a significant benefit to a local religious institution or nonprofit organization. Such gifts might include stocks, bonds, mutual fund shares, real property, or tangible property. Transfer of ownership will often require some form of legal document. There are special Internal Revenue Service rules for valuing and reporting non-cash gifts. The tax-deductible value of some gifts will be limited to the person's cost basis or the fair market value (whichever is lower). You will be allowed to deduct the full value of some gifts (including all appreciation), and will avoid any tax on capital gain. Any property given during life will be removed from the estate, and will not be subject to probate or the federal estate tax.

Author's note: Elder Law and Estate Planning Attorney K. Gabriel Heiser, J.D. has given permission to excerpt the following from his book, How to Protect Your Family's Assets from Devastating Nursing Home Costs: Medicaid Secrets.

Even when you've gathered all the information you can, and made what you thought were adequate preparations, all kinds of complications can arise.

Consider the following scenario: Joe's stepfather experienced health problems that required he be hospitalized and made Joe's mother a primary caregiver. This required Joe and his wife to become primary caregivers to his 93-year-old paternal grandmother who had been living with his parents and suffered from Alzheimer's disease. Joe faced a number of issues: because he and his wife both have to work, he needed to find someone to take care of his children. He wanted to get his grandmother on Medicaid, but she had given all her money to her children, thinking she could qualify for Medicaid by getting rid of her assets. Unfortunately, because of the five-year look-back period, she was disqualified for benefits and would have to wait for five years from that distribution. What are Joe's options? How can he make sure all three generations of his family are adequately cared for?

You're probably thinking that there are many, many details related to both estate planning and health care decision. Family situations can become very complicated so it's impossible to give a blanket answer to all the variables of family circumstances.

"Life is not measured by the number of breaths we take,
but by the moments that take our breath away."
— Unknown

"If you want to feel rich, just count the
things you have that money can't buy."
— Proverbs

Estate planning may seem like a giant mystery—but it doesn't have to be. Visit the link below to download *"The 12 Secrets of Estate Planning."*

http://krismillermoneymaestro.com/12secrets
Visit my website at: http://ReadyforPREtirement.com to learn more.

Chapter 3

LONG TERM CARE OPTIONS—
PROTECTION OF ASSETS

*"Glory lies in the attempt to reach
one's goal and not in reaching it."*
— **Mahatma Gandhi**

Seven of every ten seniors in America will end up using long term care, intermediate care, custodial care, skilled nursing care, and/or home health care, according to the Government Accounting Office in Washington, D.C. *Seven out of every ten seniors.* That's 70 percent of the entire senior population! This means you have a 70 percent chance of using long term care services. It could be only three days or as much as ten years. Do you realize that the chance of people over the age of 65 getting into a car accident is only one of every three hundred seniors? The chance of people over the age of 65 whose house may have a fire is only one of every 1,350. Yet, the chance of requiring long term care is seven of every ten seniors. You insure your home; you insure your car—but what about catastrophic illness?

Each year, the costs of catastrophic illness deplete the entire life savings of millions of senior citizens, leaving the at-home spouse with little means to continue a comfortable lifestyle (and it is much worse for single seniors).

Each year, catastrophic illness also robs children of their inheritance. Today, dealing with the need for long term care for catastrophic illnesses is the number one problem facing seniors. Will it devastate and rob you and your family of your life savings? Will it remove your dignity and freedom in your remaining years?

Overlapping options for dealing with this problem financially include:

- insurance
- annuities
- reverse mortgages

Option 1: Purchase Insurance

Here's how nursing house insurance works. First, you can select the benefit period, which is how long the coverage will last and/or pay for your care (two years, three years, lifetime, etc.; the shorter the benefit period, the lower your premiums). Remember that the average stay in a nursing home is three to five years. However, don't count on this being your situation because some may enter a nursing home for 30 days, and for others it could be many years.

Home health care insurance costs less than nursing home insurance and is easier to qualify for, in terms of your health condition, than nursing home insurance. Home health care involves having a licensed nurse, possibly supplemented by nursing assistants, come to your house and help you or a spouse with a variety of medically related services, as prescribed by your doctor. It can be a tremendous help, though there are both positive and negative aspects. Most people prefer to receive care in their homes rather than in a nursing home, but if you need 24-hour care, home health care may not be adequate. Most insurance, including Medicare and Medicaid, does not pay for more than a few hours a week of nursing visits.

Why Should I Get Long Term Care Insurance?

This much is certain:

- We are living longer.
- As we grow older, the need for assistance becomes greater.
- Odds are significant that at some point you will need long term care.
- Long term care is expensive.

What Are Your Options?

Generally, these are the most common choices:

- do nothing and rely upon government programs such as Medicare or Medicaid
- traditional long term care insurance
- self-insure

Let's Review Each of These Options

1. *Do nothing and rely upon government programs such as Medicare or Medicaid*

Medicare will only cover up to 100 days in a nursing home following a three-day hospital stay. According to the U.S. Department of Health and Human Services National Clearinghouse for Long Term Care Information, Medicare paid only 20.4 percent of the total national long term care cost in 2005.

Medicaid qualifications and coverage vary from state to state, but it is usually for those who have little or no personal assets. Medicaid paid 48.9 percent of the total national long term care cost in 2005. In general, the cost of Medicaid is poverty.

- Medicaid deductible = all your assets
- Medicaid premium = all your income

Medicaid has other disadvantages:

- loss of options
- loss of independence
- not portable from state to state

2. *Traditional long term care insurance*
   Advantages:
- transfers financial risk
- insures your estate (protects assets)
- helps avoid last-minute planning
- can help keep you out of a nursing home

   Disadvantages:
- sometimes expensive
- sometimes difficult to qualify

3. *Self-insure—use current assets*
   Advantages:
- no premiums to pay
- no underwriting

   Disadvantages:
- all your assets are exposed to long term care risk

There is a way to self-insure long term care so that your money is safe, free from market risk, liquid, grows tax-deferred, and worth three times its value for long term care needs. All you need to do is change the way you save.

Option 2: Protect Your Nest Egg—Buy an Annuity

Millions of seniors are placing funds into annuities because they are the only savings/investment vehicles that can change from an asset to an income. This special and unique feature is critical to the Medicaid planning process. Many CPAs, attorneys and insurance advisors are recommending annuities in lieu of nursing home insurance. In addition to the Medicaid planning aspect (explained below), with most fixed annuities your principal is completely safe, your assets liquid and you enjoy tax advantages (save federal, state, local income taxes and reduce and/or eliminate Social Security taxes), plus avoid probate and obtain very competitive returns.

When it comes to Medicaid planning, you want to use annuities which adapt to the Medicaid regulations. Now, here's the key. If you have money in annuities and should have to enter a nursing home, all you have to do is to annuitize the annuity.

This means that the asset of the dollars in the annuity becomes a guaranteed income (somewhat like a pension plan). This is important because you can adjust the income to meet state or federal qualifications.

The next choice is the elimination period. This is how much time needs to pass before your policy benefits will begin (0 days, 20 days, 100 days, etc.). The longer the elimination period, the less your premiums will be.

Another feature you must select is the daily room and board amount. This is the amount of benefits the policy will pay based upon the room and board cost. Some companies give you a daily dollar amount—for example, $90 a day, $110 a day, etc.—as a guide to determine the pool of money available, based on the features you select. (The average cost of a nursing home today is currently $200 to $500 per day.) The higher the daily benefit, the more expensive your plan.

On top of the daily room and board amount (or pool of money), you have the option of a five percent simple or compound inflation factor.

Now, the situation gets more complex. In 1993, the Omnibus Reconciliation Act (OBRA) was passed and became effective June 1, 1994. Part of this act was the establishment of Estate Recovery of Assets for those who become eligible for Medicaid. This new law demanded that all states engage in estate recovery, and since then, all states have passed laws which enable the state to place a lien on the homes of those who qualify for Medicaid. Many of these states place liens on property for Medicaid recovery during the process of convalescence.

But, isn't your home a non-countable asset and exempt? It is—when you're *applying* for Medicaid. But when you've *used* Medicaid benefits, the state can place a lien on the home to recover assets. Many states allow recovery of assets from family members (if the assets were transferred to children), which makes things worse if you have been gifting assets to your children. (Note: individuals are allowed to gift $13,000 a year to as many people as they wish without facing any tax consequences on the gift). Unfortunately, Medicaid considers these gifts as "transfer of assets" and can disqualify the nursing home applicant for the amount of time that the gift would have paid for long term care (the Ineligibility Penalty established by OBRA '93).

For example, let's say you had gifted $13,000 to a grandchild for college, and shortly afterwards used Medicaid for long term care. In California, that would be considered a fraudulent transfer.

Proper financial planning puts you in the driver's seat to choose the level at which you wish to be taxed. Many people can legally cut thousands of dollars off their income tax bill annually by using tax-deferred products. The Taxpayer Relief Act of 1997 has given you the power to choose your own taxable income tax rate: (a) less than 10 percent; (b) 10 percent; (c) 15 percent; (d) 20 percent; or (e) 25 percent.

What would you do with these tax savings? Take an extra vacation? Help a grandchild with college expenses? Pay for long term care insurance? The choice is yours. Just remember, you cannot choose what to do with this money if you are legally bound to send it to Uncle Sam.

The key to minimizing your tax liability is understanding what your needs are today and into the foreseeable future. Proper review and planning to meet those needs and a sound concept of the potential tax traps will help you build a sound financial future.

This is not tricky, illegal, or complicated. It's just smart management of your money!

Option 3: Set Up a Reverse Mortgage

A reverse mortgage is a non-recourse loan with no credit qualification and no need to pay the money back. Although this option is not ideal for everyone, keep in mind that a mortgage company will provide you with either a lump sum for your home or an income stream based upon the value of your home. The reverse mortgage company cannot kick you out of the home.

You can use the money for an annuity or long term care premiums. The mortgage company simply will sell the home upon the death of the second spouse and they'll recover the money they provided you (plus interest and fees as their profit). Any amount left over after the sale will go to your chosen beneficiaries. Again, make sure you deal with reputable companies who are experienced at using reverse mortgages.

State and Federal Government Intervention

How is our government involved in catastrophic illness? There are federal and state laws that impact what happens should you become seriously ill. It is better if you're familiar with these laws before you become ill. We'll go into detail about Medicaid below.

Half of all the seniors today receiving Medicaid (which pays for long term care only if you are at the poverty level) were not broke to begin with but ended up broke because they had to spend their assets down in order to qualify. This is called "nursing home spend-down." Once you qualify, Medicaid will provide an inflation rider on the daily room and board amount. This is a very important feature. With the cost of care in America, it is essential to provide for an automatic increase (inflation) of benefit amounts.

Almost no one wants to worry about losing their life savings or planning for their demise. But the fact is we are all going to die sometime and the majority of us will become ill before we die. But with proper planning, done in advance, you can pass along at least some of the assets you've acquired over your lifetime.

> *"Planning is bringing the future into the present*
> *so that you can do something about it now."*
> **—Alan Lakein, *How to Get Control of Your Time and Your Life***

Richard E. Middleton of National Brokers Alliance contributed the following article.

It's All About Planning

It's happened to all of us at some time in our life, having a friend or a loved one needing some form of long term care. Whether we needed that care at home or in a facility, it's expensive. Some are able to pay for it out of their income and savings, others are forced to go on the government's welfare programs (Medicaid), and others have planned for such an event by purchasing some form of long term care insurance. Regardless of how you are going to pay for the care, it's all about having a written plan of care for a long term care health event. Many of us have planned for other life changing events and have plans in place, such as purchasing life insurance for our families should we pass prematurely. Long term care planning should be viewed very similarly to how we have planned with life insurance. We care about our families and want to make sure that if we were to pass early, our families are well taken care of and that is why we buy life insurance. Well, long term care planning is very similar. We want to be sure when and if a long term care event happens, our families are prepared.

We all need a written plan of care in the event of an extended long term care health event. This will ensure that our families execute the plan the way we want to be taken care of.

Funding this plan can also be quite an undertaking. There are several ways to pay for such an event:

1. Your assets, savings and investments (you will need to make sure that your written plan includes instructions as to which of these should be liquidated first in the event you are incapacitated)
2. The government's welfare program, most notably Medicaid
3. Traditional long term care insurance
4. Hybrid long term care insurance (these are life insurance policies that have long term care riders or annuities that have long term care riders)
5. Any combination of the above—for example, many people will use some of their discretionary income to pay a portion of long term care expenses and have a long term care policy pay the difference

Far too often families are torn apart because a written plan of care was not in place thus leaving the decision to one child or the children. Families often find themselves in disagreement with the best plan for a family member, which never ends well. This can all be avoided when a well thought out plan of care is in place with the details of where this individual would like to receive care and how it is to be paid for.

Learn why long term care (LTC) insurance makes sense.
Go to the following link to download *"Long Term Care: Who Pays?"*
http://krismillermoneymaestro.com/common-LTC
Learn more at: http://ReadyForPREtirement.com

Chapter 4

MEDICAID PLANNING— ENTITLEMENT PROGRAMS

"It is better to light a candle than to curse the darkness."
— **Chinese proverb**

E*lder Law and Estate Planning Attorney K. Gabriel Heiser, J.D., has given permission to excerpt this chapter from his book,* How to Protect Your Family's Assets from Devastating Nursing Home Costs: Medicaid Secrets *(Phylius Press, 3rd edition, © 2009, available at www.MedicaidSecrets.com).*

In the United States, various entitlement programs are available, depending on your circumstances. The three most common programs are:

- Social Security
- Medicare
- Medicaid

Social Security: Established by the Social Security Act of 1935, this program is designed to provide income to seniors and the disabled. Funded by taxes levied on employees, employers, and the self-employed, Social Security income is based on lifetime earnings and available when you either become disabled or reach the federally mandated age of retirement, which depends on when you were born. Partial Social Security payments can be received from age 62 on, but your monthly Social Security income will be frozen at that level for the rest of your life.

Medicare: This is the popular name for the federal health insurance program for those who have turned age 65 or become disabled. The program began in 1966 and was first administered by the Social Security Administration in 1977. Later, the Medicare program was transferred to the newly created Health Care Financing Administration (HCFA).

What does Medicare pay for skilled nursing home care?

First 20 Days	Next 80 Days	After 100 Days
Medicare pays 100 percent of approved amounts	Medicare pays all except for the co-payment. Medicare Supplements will generally pay the co-payment.	Medicare pays nothing. You pay all the costs.

Medicaid: This is a federal and state program usually operated by the state health departments within the guidelines issued by HCFA. Medicaid is based solely on a person's need and income, and furnishes at least five basic services:

- inpatient hospital care
- outpatient hospital care
- physician's services
- skilled nursing home services for adults
- home health care
- laboratory and radiology services

Patient classifications that are not covered by normal health insurance:

Intermediate care: No medical necessity but still requiring attention of a RN or LPN nurse (for example, a diabetes patient requiring dressing changes or insulin treatments).

Custodial care: Includes any assistance with activities of daily living (ADLs) such as eating, drinking, toileting, bathing, ambulating, or transferring to and from bed.

What is Medicaid?

Medicaid is a joint federal-state program for the medical care of certain needy populations within the United States. Although established by federal law, the Medicaid program is for the most part administered by the individual states. The cost is shared by the federal government and the states, with the federal government paying between 50 percent and 83 percent of the cost (it pays more to poorer states, less to the wealthier states).

What makes this area of the law so complicated is that under the federal statutes there are many options given to the states as to what they will pay for and who is entitled to coverage. As a result, you have 50 different versions of the Medicaid rules, with each state selecting a different combination of options, and each one interpreting the same laws differently. That leaves the residents and attorneys in each state scratching their heads trying to figure out what they can and cannot do, to qualify for Medicaid coverage. Unfortunately, you cannot simply ask the government for an advance ruling or interpretation, like you can with the IRS. That forces you to try something first and hope for the best. If you're challenged by the state Medicaid authorities, you can appeal their interpretation if you disagree with it, and even take them to court. Of course, very few people are willing to do that, because of the significant expense and hassle involved in such a lawsuit. Consequently, that leaves you relying on your best guess of what you—and your lawyer—think the state rules actually are.

What Is Covered by Medicaid?

Once you have been approved for Medicaid, virtually all of your medical bills will be paid by the program. This includes your prescription drugs, hospital stays, nursing care, etc. Medicare may overlap this coverage, but one way or another your medical bills will be paid for you. Those who are receiving both Medicaid and Medicare coverage are known as "dual eligible." Prescription drugs, formerly paid for by Medicaid, now are paid for by Medicare Part D.

The following services must be offered by all states:

- inpatient hospital services
- outpatient hospital services
- physician services
- medical and surgical dental services
- nursing facility services for individuals age 21 or older
- home health care for persons eligible for nursing facility services
- lab and x-ray services
- family nurse practitioner services

The following services are optional, but most states will offer them, also:

- ambulatory services to individuals entitled to institutional care
- home health services to individuals entitled to nursing facility services
- prescribed drug coverage
- optometrist services and eyeglasses
- prosthetic devices
- dental services
- in-home assistance

Care in Your Home

If you are living in your home, i.e., not in a nursing home, the Medicaid program refers to you as living "in the community," and Medicaid will still pay for certain services if you qualify. Many states have a program called "HCBS," which stands for "Home and Community Based Services." Until recently, a state wishing to provide certain kinds of Medicaid assistance to elderly people, outside the nursing home, had to apply to the federal government for a specific "waiver" of the usual Medicaid rules. All states are now eligible to offer this program without first having to obtain a federal waiver. Hopefully, this will expand the access to HCBS nationally. In any event, you must check to see if your state currently offers this program to its residents or plans to do so shortly.

In general, HCBS will pay for the following in-home services:

- case management
- personal care services
- respite care services (i.e., care for the patient in a nursing home for a few days, to give the home caregiver a needed break)
- adult day health services
- homemaker/home health aide services
- habilitation (i.e., assisting people in furthering their skills in the areas of mobility, social behaviors, self care, basic safety, housekeeping, personal hygiene, health care, and financial management)

States are now able to offer to those who are already in a nursing home the option of living in the community, allowing them the ability to interact with their family and community away from the institutional setting. They will be able to have the same level of care and be covered by Medicaid. Be sure to check if your state has implemented this new program or plans to do so shortly.

Assisted Living

In most states, it is possible to have Medicaid pay for certain services even if you are living in an assisted living facility. These are under the HCBS program described above. Note that the facility must be "Medicaid certified," so you will want to make sure about that when you are searching for a facility to move into. *Note, however, that the facility's cost of basic room and board will not be paid for by Medicaid, as it would be if you resided in a nursing home.*

Nursing Homes

Medicaid will pay the full nursing home bill, including room, board, and all nursing care costs. However, it is very important to note that although 58 percent of all nursing home beds in the United States are filled with patients on the Medicaid program, not every nursing home accepts Medicaid payments. Thus, it is extremely important that you find out before you sign up for a nursing home whether it accepts Medicaid patients. While it is against the law for a nursing home to evict you because you run out of money and must go from private pay to Medicaid, that does not apply if the nursing home does not accept Medicaid from anyone! Be sure to ask! It is very upsetting to the nursing home resident to have to relocate from one nursing home to another, after finally accepting the fact that they are in a nursing home for good, have gotten used to the routines, made friends, become acquainted with the nurses, etc.

"Be the flame, not a moth."
— **Giacomo Casanova**

Applying for Benefits

Applying too late can mean that the opportunity to have the government pay for your family member's care will be lost, costing your family thousands of dollars. Although in most states it is permissible to apply for benefits for the period starting up to three months prior to the date of application, you cannot go back any further than that (see "Retroactive Coverage"). Thus, it makes sense to apply as soon as you are sure your family member can qualify.

Applying too early can be a very expensive mistake if gifts have been made that affect eligibility! Most gifts made by the Medicaid applicant and/or spouse can cause a period of disqualification if either or both of them apply for Medicaid within five years of the gift (depending on the date made; see "Transferring Assets" for a detailed explanation). Applying before this look-back period has expired can cause a huge increase in the penalty period.

Example: On March 1, 2006, John made a transfer to his children of his house, worth $250,000. If he waits until March 1, 2011 to apply for Medicaid, there will be no period of disqualification, because his gift was made outside of the five-year look-back period. However, if he applies for Medicaid on February 1, 2011, he could be disqualified from receiving Medicaid coverage for 50 months or more, depending in which state he resides.

Sometimes it makes sense to apply during the look-back period because you want to get the penalty period running. This technique, called the "Half-A-Loaf" plan, is explained in more detail in the book *How to Protect Your Family's Assets from Devastating Nursing Home Costs: Medicaid Secrets.*

The rule is, never apply until you're sure your family member qualifies, or if you are certain you want the penalty period to start immediately. In any event, if any gifts have been made within the last five years, the opinion of an experienced elder law attorney should be sought prior to actually applying for Medicaid, to make sure the time is right to do so.

Where to Apply

Every state has a system in place to permit you to apply for Medicaid benefits. The best way to find out where you need to go is to contact the social services agency in your state that deals with nursing home Medicaid eligibility. The application form will require you to list your current income and assets. You will also need to bring in your bank account records going back anywhere from six months to as much as five years. You may have to provide copies of deeds, trusts, and insurance policies.

Some states are now requiring Medicaid applicants to produce a copy of every check that they have written in the last five years. Checks written as Christmas gifts, Easter gifts, birthday gifts, or church donations could be cause for the applicant to be disqualified. However, if the gifts were made exclusively for a purpose other than to qualify for Medicaid, the gifts must be ignored. Thus, it is a good idea to start gathering the necessary information in advance of your application. Otherwise, your inability to provide the necessary documents or information could result in the imposition of a penalty period for such gifts; at the least, it could cause a delay in the processing of your application, which in turn could cause you to lose valuable benefits.

Retroactive Coverage

It is possible to apply for Medicaid coverage for a period beginning up to three months prior to the date of application. If the applicant would have qualified for Medicaid as of such date had he or she applied at such time, then the applicant will be covered starting on such date. (A state may even cover the applicant as of the first day of that month.) For example, if you thought you would not qualify for Medicaid for several months and then found out you actually could have qualified, you can apply for Medicaid immediately and ask for coverage going back up to three months. Unfortunately, the period of time before the three-month date will not be covered by Medicaid, even if you could have qualified had you applied back then. Thus it is very important to apply as soon as you are qualified; once that three-month retroactive window closes, your family may wind up having to pay privately for your care when you could have gotten Medicaid to pay all of your nursing home expenses.

NOTE: At least one state (Massachusetts) has eliminated the right of a person in a nursing home to obtain Medicaid coverage retroactively to the date of application for Medicaid. As just mentioned, the general rule under federal law is to permit three months of retroactive coverage. However, this state obtained a waiver to deviate from this federal requirement.

IMPORTANT: Thus, to be on the safe side, be sure to apply for Medicaid as soon as possible, which may even be before admission to a nursing home in some cases—assuming the applicant would otherwise qualify!

Documentation of Citizenship

As of July 1, 2006, anyone applying for or receiving Medicaid needs to prove that they are either a U.S. citizen, or national, or a qualified alien. Such proof must be made at the time of applying for Medicaid for the first time, or upon the first re-determination of eligibility (which is done once a year following initial approval) for those already receiving Medicaid coverage. It is only done once per person.

Such proof may only be made by one or more of the following:

- U.S. passport
- Certificate of Naturalization (Form N-550 or N-570)
- Certificate of U. S. Citizenship (Form N-560 or N-561)
- a valid state-issued driver's license or ID document BUT ONLY if the state requires proof of U.S. citizenship prior to issuance or obtains and verifies the individual's Social Security Number

If none of the above is available, then the applicant can provide any of the following to establish citizenship:

- U.S. birth certificate
- other evidence of U.S. citizenship if born abroad, adopted, etc.

If none of the above is available, there are still other methods allowed, in rare circumstances, such as hospital records, census records, medical records, and written affidavit if all else fails.

If one of the first four methods listed above cannot be used, then the applicant must also submit one of the following to establish identity:

- a valid state-issued driver's license with photo or other identifying information
- school ID card with photo
- U.S. military card or draft record
- government ID card with photo or other ID information. All identification must either be originals or copies certified by the issuing agency; notarized copies are not acceptable.
- such other documentation as the Secretary of Health and Human Services may allow by regulation (For complete details, you can search online for "Medicaid citizenship guidelines" to find the final rules issued by the Centers for Medicare & Medicaid Services [CMS].)

Because it may take some time to obtain the above documentation, particularly if one of the first four methods of proof is unavailable, the family should assist the prospective Medicaid applicant in getting this documentation together as soon as possible.

Nursing Home Bills During the Application Period

Once you apply for Medicaid, the nursing home where you are staying may not make you pay the nursing home bill until the application process is complete and you are determined to be ineligible to receive Medicaid. If you are approved, then the nursing home will be able to apply to Medicaid for the back charges. If you are denied and then appeal the denial, the nursing home may be able to charge you during the period of the appeal process, but if you are ultimately approved for Medicaid, the nursing home will have to refund to your family all the fees it received from your family during the appeals process.

Since it can be difficult and time-consuming to get the nursing home to refund money you already paid them, you should always try not to pay the nursing home during the initial application period. Remember, you are not responsible for paying the nursing home during this period—by law, they have to wait.

Medical Qualification Rules

In addition to the strict financial rules noted here, there are also medical qualifications to meet before a person will be eligible for Medicaid coverage for a nursing home stay. The applicant must prove he or she is at least age 65, blind, or disabled. According to the federal regulations, to be disabled means that you are unable "to do any substantial gainful activity by reason of any medically determinable physical or mental impairment that can be expected to result in death or which has lasted or can be expected to last for a continuous period of not less than 12 months."

Typically, the state will send a nurse or trained intake worker to the Medicaid applicant's home to interview the applicant. The nurse or worker will have a checklist of activities of daily living (ADLs), and in order to be deemed "sick" enough to qualify for Medicaid, the applicant must "fail" a certain number of these tests. Obviously, this is not a time for the applicant to downplay his or her disabilities; such comments can cause the nurse or worker to think the applicant is actually in better shape than he or she really is, with the result that Medicaid coverage will be denied. If that happens, the applicant's only recourse at that point is to begin an expensive appeals process.

Meeting the medical qualifications is not typically an issue when you are looking at a frail elderly or Alzheimer's patient. The real issues are more often that of having too much income or too many assets, so let's move on and take a detailed look at that.

Income Qualification Rules

Unmarried: As of November 2010, an unmarried individual may not have more than $2,022 of income per month. (This figure, published by the federal government, changes annually to reflect cost-of-living changes.) "Income" for these purposes includes both "earned" income (wages) and "unearned" income (interest and dividends).

What if your income exceeds this amount? There are actually two different ways this is handled, depending on the state in which you live.

Income-Cap States

In an "income-cap" state, if your income is even one dollar above the limit, you are initially disqualified from Medicaid. (At the time of this writing, approximately 20 states are "income-cap" states.) A problem arises if you earn too much money to qualify for Medicaid to help you pay the nursing home bill, but not enough to pay for it privately! It was this exact dilemma that led to the lawsuit that finally created the solution: all these states now allow you to set up a simple trust and have your income paid to the trust. The trust then takes the income and pays it to the nursing home each month. A family member can act as the Trustee of this trust, keeping the costs down. Assuming you follow some basic rules about this process, your excess income will not prevent you from qualifying for Medicaid, unless your income exceeds the amount that Medicaid would otherwise pay to the nursing home each month for your care.

This type of trust is known as a "Qualified Income Trust" or "Miller Trust" (after the case, *Miller v Ibarra*, discussed earlier, that established this trust procedure). Check to see if your state publishes a standard, short-form trust that is essentially a "fill-in-the-blanks" document. Using such a form means you don't have to hire an attorney to create this trust document for you.

In each of the following examples, assume that the individual applying for Medicaid is single, is already in a nursing home, and has minimal assets.

Example 1: Sam has only his Social Security income of $900 to live on. He will qualify for Medicaid. Each month, his Social Security check goes to the nursing home, and Medicaid picks up the balance of his bill.

Example 2: Martin has Social Security income of $1,200 and a small monthly pension of $900. He will also qualify for Medicaid, but since his total income of $2,100 exceeds $2,022 (the income upper limit to avoid needing a trust), a Qualified Income Trust will have to be set up to receive the $2,100 each month. That income is then paid over to the nursing home, and once again Medicaid will pay the balance of the bill.

Example 3: Mary has Social Security, a pension, and some oil lease income that together total $6,000 per month. In the state where Mary lives, that's actually more than the cost of her monthly nursing home bill, so she will not qualify for Medicaid because her income is just too high. Is there a way for her to reduce her income? She is unable to assign her Social Security or pension to another family member, since those are non-assignable under the law. However, she can probably assign her oil lease interest, which would carry the income with it to the new owner. Of course, such assignment is a gift and will cause a penalty period (see discussion of gifts, below). However, it is an option that should be considered and discussed with the elder law attorney who will assist Mary to qualify for Medicaid.

Spend-Down States

The balance of the states permit the nursing home resident to spend down his or her monthly income (on medical expenses and, as most of these states allow, on nursing home costs), with Medicaid paying the shortfall. In other words, so long as the income of the applicant is below the actual cost of the nursing home, the applicant can qualify for Medicaid (assuming the applicant also meets the asset test).

Married: The treatment of income of a married couple is vastly more complicated than that of a single individual. That is because of the various attribution rules that permit the income of the Nursing Home Spouse to be shifted to the spouse still residing in the community (i.e., the "Community Spouse"). As a result of this opportunity, there is much planning that can be done to maximize the income of the Community Spouse and minimize the income of the Nursing Home Spouse.

Income for married couples is treated according to this rule: when one spouse of a married couple applies for Medicaid, "the name on the check determines whose income it is." A payment of annuity or pension income to one spouse is deemed that spouse's income only.

If you and your spouse own property jointly, then any income from that property will be deemed to be earned by each spouse 50/50. This also applies to joint bank accounts, payments from a trust, or a promissory note or annuity payable to both spouses. Note that this is a rebuttable presumption: if indeed all of the money in the joint account can be traced to one spouse, then it may be possible to prove that the account income should only be deemed to be that of the contributing spouse.

The important point to remember is that if you are living in the community and your spouse is in the nursing home, you will not have to contribute any portion of your income toward your spouse's nursing home bill, under the Medicaid rules.

Example: Joe, who is still living at home, has pension and Social Security income totaling $2,500 a month. His wife, Edie, now resides in a nursing home. Her income is only from Social Security and equals $450 a month. Nonetheless, once Edie is approved for Medicaid, Joe does not have to contribute one penny to her nursing home care, and he can keep his entire $2,500 each month.

Although the Community Spouse never has to contribute any of his or her income to the other spouse's care, it is possible for the Nursing Home Spouse's income to be paid to the Community Spouse. So it's a one-way street: income only flows—if at all—from the Nursing Home Spouse to the Community Spouse, and never vice versa.

That's because the Community Spouse is entitled to a minimum monthly income of between $1,821 and $2,739 (depending on the state). These figures are set by the federal government and change annually. The applicable figure for the particular state is known as the "Minimum Monthly Maintenance Needs Allowance" or "MMMNA." If the Community Spouse's income is less than the MMMNA, then a certain amount of the Nursing Home Spouse's income may be allocated to the Community Spouse, sufficient (to the extent possible) to increase the Community Spouse's income up to the MMMNA. Such allotment of income from the Nursing Home Spouse to the Community Spouse is called the "Monthly Income Allowance," or "MIA."

Example 1: Assume the Community Spouse has no income other than $500 a month from Social Security, and the Nursing Home Spouse has Social Security of $1,000 a month. Based on these numbers, the amount of the Nursing Home Spouse's income that can be shifted over to the Community Spouse—the MIA—will be $1,000. The Community Spouse will be entitled to keep all the couple's combined income, because the total of their combined income would be only $1,500 per month. Since that's less than the minimum entitlement income of $1,821, the Community Spouse can keep all of the income, and Medicaid will pay the entire nursing home bill.

MMMNA	$1,821
Community Spouse's income	(500)
Shortfall	1,321
Nursing Home Spouse's income	1,000
Amount able to be shifted (MIA)	1,000

NOTE: You can never shift more than the shortfall figure, or if less, the total amount of the Nursing Home Spouse's income. If the Nursing Home Spouse's income is less than the shortfall amount, it will be possible to increase the amount of excluded assets the Community Spouse can retain.

Example 2: Assume the Community Spouse has income of $500 a month, and the Nursing Home Spouse has income of $2,000 a month. Based on these numbers, the Community Spouse will be allowed to keep $1,321 from the Nursing Home Spouse's income, i.e., an MIA of $1,321 (which brings the Community Spouse up to $1,821). The Nursing Home Spouse will then contribute the balance of his or her income ($2,000 − $1,321 = $679) every month toward the nursing home bill. Medicaid will pick up the balance of the bill.

MMMNA	$1,821
Community Spouse's income	(500)
Shortfall	1,321
Nursing Home Spouse's income	2,000
Amount able to be shifted (MIA)	1,321

NOTE: You can never shift more than the shortfall figure.

Example 3: Assume the Community Spouse has income of $2,000 a month, and the Nursing Home Spouse has income of $500 a month. In this case, because the Community Spouse's income exceeds the MMMNA of $1,821, no portion of the Nursing Home Spouse's income is allowed to be shifted to the Community Spouse. As a result, the Nursing Home Spouse must pay all of his or her monthly income toward the nursing home bill, and Medicaid will pick up the balance of the bill, once the Nursing Home Spouse has qualified for Medicaid coverage.

MMMNA	$1,821
Community Spouse's income	(2,000)
Shortfall	-0-
Nursing Home Spouse's income	500
Amount able to be shifted (MIA)	-0-

Increasing the MMMNA

Sometimes it is possible to increase the income of the Community Spouse above the minimum amount (MMMNA), although in no case can a state permit an increase above $2,739 without either a court order of support or proof that the Community Spouse would face "significant financial duress" due to "exceptional circumstances."

There are three ways to do this: increase the MMMNA by the amount of the excess shelter allowance, apply for a Fair Hearing, or obtain a court order of support for the Community Spouse.

Excess Shelter Allowance (ESA)

In a state with an MMMNA less than the absolute maximum permitted under federal law ($2,739), it may be possible to increase the MMMNA based on high "shelter" costs. If the "shelter" costs of the Community Spouse exceed 30 percent of the MMMNA, then this excess may be added on top of the MMMNA, but only up to the maximum monthly allowance figure published by the federal government (currently $2,739). Since the current MMMNA is $1,821, 30 percent of that is $546. So if the shelter costs of the Community Spouse exceed $546, that excess amount may be added to the MMMNA when trying to figure out how much of the Nursing Home Spouse's income can be shifted over to the Community Spouse.

For these purposes, "shelter" expenses only include rent or mortgage payment, condo fees (if any), real estate taxes and homeowner's insurance, and either the standard utility allowance (currently between $198 and $720, depending on the state) or, if your state does not use such an allowance, the actual cost of utilities (heat, electricity, gas, and—in most states—telephone service). Some states even permit you to use the higher of the standard utility allowance or actual cost of utilities when calculating whether or not you qualify for the excess shelter allowance. Once again, you need to check your own state's regulations on this point.

In those few states where the standard utility allowance by itself exceeds the standard shelter allowance, the MMMNA will always be increased, at least by the amount of that excess.

Example: Mary lives at home in the community, and her husband, Joe, is in the nursing home. Mary's income is $750 a month, all from Social Security. Joe's monthly income is $2,500, from his Social Security and pension. Because Mary's income is less than $1,821, we know she is entitled to shift a portion of Joe's income to her. Ignoring shelter costs, she is entitled to $1,821 minus $750, or $1,071.

MMMNA	$1,821
Community Spouse's income	(750)
Shortfall	1,071
Nursing Home Spouse's income	2,500
Amount able to be shifted (MIA)	1,071

NOTE: You can never shift more than the shortfall figure.

Because Joe has excess income even after he shifts some of it to Mary, we should try to see if there's a way to increase the amount Mary is entitled to. After all, Joe's income will all have to go to the nursing home, where it won't do him any good: it will simply reduce the amount that Medicaid would otherwise pay the nursing home.

So the next step is to see if Mary would be entitled to more of Joe's income if her shelter costs are high enough. Here are the figures:

Condo fees	$250
Real estate taxes	150
Homeowner's insurance	100
Standard Utility Allowance	374
TOTAL	**874**
Shelter allowance	(546)
Excess Shelter Allowance	328

Because her shelter costs ($874) exceed the permitted standard shelter allowance ($546), Mary is allowed to add the excess ($874 – $546 = $328) to the MMMNA ($1,821) for an increased MMMNA of $2,149. Since her own income is $750, this means she is entitled to shift $1,399 ($2,149 – $750) from Joe's income to herself, each month. Joe's contribution to the nursing home each month will now be reduced by the same amount that is shifted over to Mary, i.e., $1,399. This process allows Mary to keep an additional $16,788 of Joe's income each year!

Summary:

MMMNA	$1,821
Excess Shelter Allowance (ESA)	328
Increased MMMNA	2,149
Community Spouse's income	(750)

Shortfall	1,399
Nursing Home Spouse's income	2,500
Amount able to be shifted (MIA)	1,399

Family Allowance

An additional amount may be deducted from the Nursing Home Spouse's income before paying the nursing home, if certain other family members are living in the home with the Community Spouse. For these purposes, the term "family member" only includes minor or dependent children, dependent parents, or dependent siblings of the Nursing Home Spouse or of the Community Spouse who are residing with the Community Spouse. To calculate this, you subtract the income of the family member from the MMMNA and divide by three. This amount will be deducted from the Nursing Home Spouse's income and paid over to the Community Spouse for the benefit of the family member. This payment does not count as part of the MMMNA, however, so it is not subject to the MMMNA cap of $2,739.

Fair Hearings

In cases where even the maximum MMMNA is not enough to cover the essential monthly living expenses of the Community Spouse, you can ask for a "Fair Hearing" before the state Medicaid agency. A Fair Hearing is an administrative appeal within the Medicaid state agency that makes the determination of financial eligibility for Medicaid. It is usually an informal proceeding, but it is a good idea to bring an attorney with you. For example, the Community Spouse may have unusually high living expenses, very high prescription drug costs, or a dependent relative living with him with expenses that exceed the family allowance. If he is successful at the Fair Hearing, he will be permitted to shift a greater amount of income from the Nursing Home Spouse to himself each month.

The test is whether the Community Spouse needs income above even the maximum MMMNA, "due to exceptional circumstances resulting in significant financial duress."

For example, if the Community Spouse lives in assisted living or at home with full-time home health care, the costs can easily exceed $4,000 per month. In such a case, there is a good argument for an increased MMMNA, and requesting a Fair Hearing would be the way to do this.

Court Order of Support

If the maximum MMMNA is still insufficient to meet the monthly income needs of the Community Spouse, the Community Spouse can petition the local court for an Order of Support. The Order will set forth the amount of income that the Nursing Home Spouse must pay each month to the Community Spouse. This Order must be recognized by the Medicaid agency. The petition to the court should be done prior to applying for Medicaid, but may be done before or after the "resource assessment."

Asset Qualification Rules

Although there are strict limits as to how much money and other assets a person or married couple may have in order to qualify for Medicaid, not all assets will count against the Medicaid applicant. Certain assets are countable, some are deemed unavailable, and others are specifically excluded by statute.

In determining if one spouse of a married couple can qualify for Medicaid, the state Medicaid agency will consider all assets of both spouses, whether owned separately or jointly, according to the rules below, and then determine if they are countable, unavailable, or excluded. The Community Spouse will then be allowed to "protect" a certain amount of the countable assets (as more fully explained at "Married," below).

Valuation

In determining what value your various assets have for purposes of Medicaid eligibility, it is your net equity that counts. In other words, an asset's value is the price that it can reasonably be expected to sell for on the open market in the particular geographic area involved, minus any encumbrances (i.e., debt) on the asset. Note that if you have $10,000 in cash in the bank, and $10,000 in credit card debt, the debt will not be netted against the cash! You will need to pay off the debt, otherwise Medicaid will simply count that $10,000 toward your asset limit, ignoring the debt.

Countable Assets

If you can spend it or convert it to cash, it is generally countable. Here are the primary examples of "countable" assets:

- cash, checking and savings accounts
- CDs

- stocks, bonds, mutual funds
- IRA, 401(k), 403(b), TIAA-CREF, and other retirement-type accounts (with exceptions discussed below)
- life insurance cash values (if the total face value of all policies—other than term insurance and burial insurance—exceeds $1,500)
- annuities not yet in pay status
- all autos beyond the first car
- trucks, tractors, boats, machinery, livestock
- buildings and land that are not specifically excluded

Unavailable Assets

Certain types of assets are non-countable, because they are not legally accessible to you:

- an interest in someone's estate, prior to distribution
- a lawsuit you've filed, prior to the judgment
- real estate that cannot be sold because of legal technicalities

Excluded Assets

Certain assets, while still available and accessible to you, are nonetheless considered "excluded" or "exempt," i.e., they will not affect your eligibility for Medicaid.

$2,000 Cash: Regardless of whether you are single or married, if you are successful in qualifying for Medicaid coverage you may retain up to $2,000 in cash or other countable assets. In any month where your assets exceed $2,000, however, you could be disqualified and lose Medicaid coverage. This could be a very costly mistake so you need to be careful always to keep the bank account of the Medicaid recipient well below the $2,000 limit!

The Home: The general rule is a $500,000 exclusion. If you are single, and your principal place of residence is a house or condo, it is an excluded asset, so long as your equity interest in the residence does not exceed the state limit (at least $500,000, but this amount can be increased up to $750,000 under federal law, if the state you are in so chooses; most have not done so). The home used to be excluded no matter its value, but that changed with the Deficit Reduction Act (DRA) of 2005, effective January 1, 2006 (note this date, which is earlier than the effective date of February 8, 2006, for most other DRA provisions).

Note that it is the value of your equity interest, not the value of the home itself, that is critical. In other words, if you and your brother are equal joint owners of the house you live in, and the home has been appraised at $800,000, your equity interest is only one-half of that, i.e., $400,000, so you are under the limit. Of course, if you were the sole owner, then you'd be over the limit. If the value of your equity interest in your home is above the state limit, in order for the home to be excluded you will need to reduce your equity interest.

If the value of your equity interest in your home is under the state limit when you first apply for Medicaid, the home will be an excluded asset. But be aware that if the value of your home has increased above the state limit at the time of your annual redetermination, the home will no longer be excluded and you can lose your Medicaid coverage! Thus, it is extremely important for your family to keep track of the value of your home, and if it looks like it's getting over the state limit, you'll need to implement one of the options discussed earlier, to reduce your equity interest.

If you are married and your spouse resides in the home, or you have a child (under age 21, or blind or permanently disabled) living in your home, then it is excluded no matter what its value.

Scope of the Exclusion: Both the dwelling and the land underneath it qualify for the home exclusion. You do not need to own the dwelling: you can be living in someone else's trailer on your land, and the land will be excluded under the home exclusion.

The home itself, the land the home sits on, all contiguous land, and related outbuildings are all covered by the exclusion. (If the adjoining lot is across the street from your house, it still qualifies as being contiguous.) So a house and attached farm can all be excluded. Of course, there is still the $500,000 exclusion limitation (unless one of the exceptions applies: spouse or child—under age 21, or blind or permanently disabled—living in the home).

A mobile home or a houseboat both qualify for the home exclusion.

"Intent to Return": If you have to move out of your home and into a nursing home, the home will continue to be an excluded asset under the rules discussed above, with the same limitations, if you have the intent to return to your home should you ever become well enough to leave the nursing home. This rule applies no matter how unlikely it is that you'll ever recover to the point where you are

able to leave the nursing home. If you are incapacitated to the point where you are unable to communicate your intent to return home, a spouse or dependent relative is permitted to express your intent on your behalf. However, to be on the safe side, it is a good idea for you—as soon as you move out of your home into a nursing home—to sign a statement explicitly stating that if you are ever well enough, your intent is to return to residing in your old home. This can be useful to show to the Medicaid authorities should it become necessary to document your intent to return.

What if you leave your home of many years and move to an assisted living facility and then later into a nursing home? Will the former home still be excluded? No, since the former home is no longer your principal place of residence. Obviously, a short hospital stay in between the transition from your home to a nursing home will not cause you to lose the home exclusion. But any reasonable time where you moved your permanent residence from your old home to a new home, apartment, or assisted living facility, could certainly prevent your former home from being an excluded asset. The key test is if you continued to "intend to return" to your former home. For example, the regulations of some states provide that the home will no longer be excluded if you moved out more than six months before you entered the nursing home. Of course, if your spouse or child (under age 21, or blind or permanently disabled) remains in your old home, it will continue to be excluded regardless of whether you go directly from that home to a nursing home.

Sale of the Home: If you or your spouse sells the home, the proceeds from the sale will continue to be excluded so long as they are reinvested in another excluded home within three months of the sale. Whatever is not reinvested will become countable. Thus, if you are single, those extra proceeds could cause you to lose your Medicaid eligibility. If you are married and on Medicaid, and at the time of sale the house is titled solely in the name of the Community Spouse, the extra proceeds may be safely retained by the Community Spouse and will not cause you (the Nursing Home Spouse) to become ineligible for Medicaid. That's because of the federal statute that states that the assets of the Community Spouse cannot be deemed available to the Nursing Home Spouse starting with the month after the month in which the Nursing Home Spouse is declared eligible for Medicaid coverage.

One Automobile: One automobile of any value is excluded. Until recently, an auto was only excluded up to $4,500 in value, but that limitation is now gone. Once you go past that first car, additional vehicles will be countable assets, at their fair market value (less any outstanding car loan). See *Medicaid Secrets* for some planning ideas related to cars.

Personal Property: Under the federal regulations as amended on March 9, 2005, all household goods (furniture, furnishings, TV, computer, etc.) and personal effects (jewelry, clothing, etc.) are now excluded when determining a person's Medicaid eligibility. This is so regardless of their value. "Household goods" must be items of personal property found in or near a home, that are used on a regular basis, or items needed by the householder for maintenance, use and occupancy of the premises as a home. "Personal effects" are considered items of personal property that ordinarily are worn or carried by the individual, or are articles that otherwise have an intimate relation to the individual. Items with religious or cultural significance are also excluded under these rules. Items held for investment purposes, though, are not excluded and their value will be counted: these include gems, jewelry that is not worn or held for family significance, recently purchased expensive artwork, and other collectibles.

How will the Medicaid workers know whether your household goods, furniture, etc., are normal household items, or if such items are really "held for investment" or "collectibles"? According to the federal regulations, "We will not routinely examine all of an individual's furniture and personal possessions to determine if any pieces are valuable artwork or antiques, [but] we will have the regulatory authority to count such value items as resources when we become aware of such items."

While it is true that your wedding ring and other personal jewelry are excluded, do not run out and purchase expensive jewelry and expect it to be excluded. This was tried in a famous Massachusetts case, where the individual in question, in an attempt to qualify for Medicaid, purchased a $45,000 diamond ring. Unfortunately, the judge ruled that this jewelry item was not excluded but was a countable investment asset. So the moral of the story is, don't get greedy!

Funeral and Burial Funds:

Bank Account: Up to $1,500 may be placed in a bank account, revocable account, trust or other arrangement, and if it is designated as a burial fund, it will be excluded from your countable assets. However, this exclusion must be reduced by (1) the amount of any irrevocable burial funds such as that described in the next section, and (2) the face value of any life insurance policy whose cash value is excluded (see "Life Insurance," below). For a married couple, the $1,500 exclusion applies to each spouse.

Prepaid Funeral/Burial: There is no practical limit to the amount you can set aside in a prepaid burial and funeral account established with a funeral home or in an irrevocable trust earmarked only for payment of your funeral and burial expenses. With a funeral home, the money must either be placed in an escrow account or trust account by the funeral home. Some states require that the contract specifically state that any funds in the account not ultimately used for funeral and burial expenses following your death must be paid to the state if you were on Medicaid. In any event, you should not put more into such an account than you believe you will actually need to pay for these expenses; having any sort of prearranged "deal" with the funeral home to pay the excess to your family is clearly illegal.

Life Insurance: Life insurance earmarked for burial expenses ("burial insurance"), where the proceeds can only be used for burial expenses, is an excluded asset.

Family Coverage: Not only can you prepay funeral and burial expenses for yourself (and your spouse, if any), but you are also permitted to prepay the burial space costs for the following family members: your children (of any age), stepchildren, adopted children, brothers, sisters, parents, adoptive parents, and the spouses of any of those persons. This includes burial plots, gravesites, crypts, mausoleums, urns, niches, and other customary and traditional repositories for the deceased's remains, provided such spaces are owned by the individual. It also includes vaults, headstones, markers, plaques, and burial containers, and arrangements for opening and closing the gravesite for the burial.

Does your everyday reality involve traffic jams, piles of paperwork, rushing to meet deadlines, and struggling to pay your bills? Wouldn't it be nice to live a peaceful, carefree lifestyle, especially in your golden years? It is possible. You just have to plan for retirement early. Today is the perfect day to start!

Go to the following link to download "*Retirement: The Journey to Freedom.*"
http://krismillermoneymaestro.com/journeytofreedom
For more information see: http://ReadyForPREtirement.com.

IRA Investments

If the Medicaid applicant is unmarried, then the IRA or other retirement asset (such as 401(k), 403(b), etc.) is countable, the same as cash. Some states recognize that if the retirement assets were withdrawn to pay bills, there would be a substantial income tax due on the withdrawn amount. Accordingly, those states will reduce the "countable" amount by an estimated amount of the tax, e.g., 20 percent. If no such reduction is permitted in your state, you may be better off withdrawing the entire amount of the retirement assets and paying the taxes immediately as an estimated tax, since otherwise Medicaid will ignore the amount of taxes you will owe on that withdrawal come next year once you file your income tax return, in effect over-valuing your retirement assets by the amount of the tax you'll owe. If the withdrawal will kick you into a higher tax bracket, try to withdraw half this year and half on January 2 of next year; that will divide the taxable distributions between two tax years, possibly saving you some money.

If the Medicaid applicant is married, many states do not count the retirement assets of the Community Spouse. In these states, then, the Community Spouse may retain the $109,560 Community Spouse Resource Allowance (CSRA) in addition to any retirement assets. Other states are not so generous and count the retirement assets of both spouses the same as cash in the bank.

Property Used in a Trade or Business

According to federal law, real or personal property "essential to self-support"—that is, currently used in a trade or business—is excluded from resources regardless of its value or rate of return. For example, if you have a working farm, the land, tool sheds, livestock and equipment would all be excluded. A small family-owned business would also qualify under this exclusion. This seems to have little application to an unmarried individual who is in a nursing home, since such person will of course not be able to argue that he or she is currently using such property for self-support. However, for a married couple, it could exclude a significant amount of property so long as it is still in current use by the Community Spouse in a trade or business or as an employee. Unfortunately, many states have ignored this rule or limited it to the $6,000/6 percent amount discussed below, which should only be applied to non-business property.

Non-Business Property Used for Self-Support

If real or personal property is not used in a trade or business, only the first $6,000 of value is excluded, if it generates at least a 6 percent return on the amount excluded.

Example: If you own a separate lot of land worth $10,000, and you rent it out to someone who moved his own mobile home onto the lot, as long as it generates at least $600 of income each year, $6,000 of the land's value may be excluded (the income must be prorated to the entire lot).

Life Insurance

Only the cash value of a life insurance policy owned by the Medicaid applicant is counted; thus, all term life insurance policies are ignored. Also, if the total face value of all life insurance policies—other than term insurance and burial insurance—is less than $1,500, then the cash value is ignored.

If you are applying for Medicaid and already have a term policy in effect, you won't be able to divert any of your income to keep that policy in force, once you are on Medicaid. If your family realizes that your life expectancy is reduced and thus it makes sense not to let the policy lapse, they should consider paying the annual premiums themselves, out of their own pockets. It is also advisable to transfer ownership of the policy to another family member, so that family member will be the one to receive premium notices, etc.

Married: Community Spouse Resource Allowance (CSRA)

The basic rules discussed above as to when an asset is counted, unavailable or excluded apply to married couples and unmarried individuals alike. In either case, the person applying for Medicaid cannot have more than $2,000 in countable assets. The big difference is that under the Medicaid rules the Community Spouse is allowed to own a certain amount of assets (i.e., resources) that do not count against the $2,000 that the Nursing Home Spouse is permitted to own. This "protected amount" is known as the Community Spouse Resource Allowance, or CSRA. All other countable assets owned by the couple, regardless of which spouse owns the asset, must be "spent down," converted into non-countable assets, or otherwise disposed of by the couple, before the Nursing Home Spouse will be eligible for Medicaid.

Let's take a look at how the CSRA is determined.

"Snapshot" Rule

Regardless of whether a married nursing home resident applies for Medicaid immediately upon entering the nursing home or some months later, the CSRA is based on the value of the couple's assets as of the date the Nursing Home Spouse first entered the nursing home. To be precise, this "snapshot" is taken on the first day of the month in which the Nursing Home Spouse is in the nursing home (or a patient in the hospital just prior to entering the nursing home, as the case may be) and likely to remain there for a continuous period of at least 30 consecutive days.

Unlike how income is separately counted for each spouse, a married couple's assets are simply added together when determining the allowable assets each spouse can keep. Thus, it doesn't matter how an asset is titled—husband's name, wife's name, or joint names—it's all treated the same for these purposes. (Note that community property rules and prenuptial and postnuptial agreements are all ignored for purposes of calculating the CSRA.)

As a practical matter, when one spouse of a married couple is in a nursing home and it appears that Medicaid assistance may be needed at some point, the Community Spouse should make an appointment with a caseworker at the local office of the state department of human services to request a "resource assessment." This is not the same as applying for Medicaid, which as a general rule should not be done until it is certain that the spouse will indeed qualify at such time (or unless you're certain you want a penalty period to start running). (For the consequences of applying for Medicaid too early, see above.) The "resource assessment" will establish the total value of a married couple's countable assets as of the "snapshot" date, for purposes of calculating the CSRA. Many couples do not request a resource assessment and instead wait until one of them applies for Medicaid. However, the more time that has passed before the resource assessment is done, the more difficult it can be to recreate the assets owned by the couple on the "snapshot" date as well as what the assets were worth at that time. Hence, it is always better to get the resource assessment done as soon as possible after a spouse enters the nursing home.

Once the total countable assets as of the snapshot date are determined, the Community Spouse is allowed to keep a portion—or in some cases all—of those assets (i.e., the CSRA). The CSRA calculation varies from state to state, as discussed below.

Fifty Percent States

In some states, the Community Spouse may protect no more than 50 percent of the total countable assets of the couple, with a minimum CSRA of $21,912 and a maximum CSRA of $109,560 (federal figures, updated annually). Some of these states round up the minimum figure to, for example, $25,000, or even set the minimum amount much higher, e.g., $75,000. To find out if your state is a "50 percent" or "100 percent" state, you may need to contact someone at your state's Medicaid eligibility department.

Example 1: Joe (at home) and Mary (in the nursing home) have a total of $23,000 in countable assets. Joe can keep the greater of $21,912 or 50 percent of their combined assets. Since 50 percent of $23,000 is less than $21,912, Joe gets to keep $21,912, and Mary can keep the balance of their assets—$1,088. Since Mary has less than $2,000, she can immediately apply for Medicaid without having to spend down any of the couple's assets.

Example 2: What if Joe and Mary had $150,000? You start by taking 50 percent of that amount, which is $75,000. Since that's more than $21,912 but less than the maximum permitted amount of $109,560, Joe can keep that $75,000, while Mary is deemed the owner of the other half, i.e., $75,000. Since Mary is only permitted to have $2,000, she would not qualify for Medicaid until her excess assets—$73,000— were disposed of in some way.

Example 3: What if Joe and Mary had $250,000, instead? Once again, you start by taking 50 percent of that amount, which is $125,000. But since that exceeds $109,560, Joe is only permitted to protect $109,560. The balance—$140,440—is deemed to be Mary's. Since Mary is only permitted to have $2,000, she would not qualify for Medicaid until her excess assets—$138,440—were disposed of in some way.

NOTE: If you reside in a "fifty percent state," and the total countable assets of you and your spouse are between $21,912 and $109,560, there is a way where you can increase the amount of your countable assets and thereby increase the CSRA. This must be done before one spouse enters the nursing home, because it must be completed before the "snapshot" date.

Hundred Percent States

In the other states, the Community Spouse may keep 100 percent of the total countable assets of the couple, up to the maximum amount (currently $109,560). There is no "minimum" CSRA in these states.

Example 1: Joe (at home) and Mary (in the nursing home) have a total of $21,000. Joe can keep all of the assets, since they're less than $109,560.

Example 2: Joe and Mary have a total of $80,000. Joe keeps not just $40,000, but the full $80,000, since that's less than $109,560.

Example 3: If Joe and Mary had $150,000, Joe keeps the first $109,560, and Mary is considered the owner of the balance—$40,440. Since Mary is only permitted to have $2,000, she would not qualify for Medicaid until her excess assets—$38,440—were disposed of in some way.

Increasing the CSRA

We have been looking at ways of calculating the default CSRA. If the couple is not satisfied with the state determination of the CSRA, it may be possible to get an increase. There are two ways to do this: apply for a Fair Hearing or obtain a court order of support for the Community Spouse.

Fair Hearing: If the income of the Community Spouse is under the MMMNA, then it is possible to request a Fair Hearing to seek an increase in the CSRA by an amount of assets sufficient to generate the additional income needed to bring the Community Spouse up to the MMMNA level. However, since the DRA's effective date of February 8, 2006, all states must use the "income first" approach in setting the CSRA. That means that the Community Spouse's income must first be increased by shifting income from the Nursing Home Spouse (to the extent possible, up to the MMMNA level) before the CSRA may be increased by this method. As a practical matter, this means that this technique can only apply if the total income of both spouses is under the MMMNA (as adjusted).

Example: Bart is in the nursing home and his only income is $500/month of Social Security. His wife, Louise, lives in the community and her only income is $1,000/month of Social Security. Under the MMMNA rules discussed above, because Louise's income is less than $1,821/month, Louise will be allowed to keep all of Bart's income. However, that still leaves her short $321/month ($1,821 −

1,000 – $500 = $321). Because of this, Louise will be entitled to keep an additional amount of the couple's assets, based on the reasoning that those additional assets will be needed to generate that additional $321/month of income.

It works like this: if Louise can only expect typically to earn 3.5 percent on her money, then it will take what amount of additional assets to generate that $321/month shortfall? The formula is:

3.5% of x = $321/month or $3,852/yr; so x = $3,852 ÷ 3.5% = $110,057.

Result: Louise can protect not just the standard CSRA of $109,560, but an additional $110,057 of the couple's assets, for a total of $219,617. Once they have reduced their assets to that level, Bart can apply for Medicaid.

Note that the 3.5 percent income figure used above is an example. Some states set the percentage you must use; others let you argue at the Fair Hearing what an appropriate percent should be, based on an average of local bank savings account or short-term CD rates, etc. (The lower the interest rate allowed, the greater the amount of additional assets the Community Spouse can keep.) Other states require you to obtain estimates of the cost of a single premium lifetime annuity sufficient to generate the income shortfall, and the average of the estimated costs of that annuity is the amount by which you can increase the CSRA (you don't actually have to buy the annuity, however). Thus, the particular rules of your state must be consulted before you go into the Fair Hearing.

If the Community Spouse were able to increase her MMMNA from the default minimum of $1,821 to the maximum of $2,739, that additional $918/month allowed income would permit the Community Spouse to protect up to an additional $314,743 of assets as part of her CSRA. Here's how the numbers work:

Maximum MMMNA	$2,739
Default MMMNA	(1,821)
Increase/month	918
Increase/year	11,016

Amount of assets required to generate $11,016/yr, at 3.5 percent interest: $314,743.

Court Order of Support: If the Community Spouse finds that he or she simply cannot make ends meet with the default minimum amounts of income or assets allowed under the Medicaid rules, the Community Spouse should seek a Court Order of Support to increase either or both of these amounts. If an Order is obtained to increase the spouse's allowed income (i.e., the MMMNA), then the next step is to request a Fair Hearing to shift additional assets under the analysis discussed above. It is also possible to obtain a Court Order to increase the CSRA itself. These Orders must be recognized by the Medicaid agency in determining the amount of income or assets the Community Spouse is entitled to keep, while still allowing the Nursing Home Spouse to qualify for Medicaid. The petition to the Court should be done prior to applying for Medicaid, but may be done before or after the "resource assessment."

A Court Order may also be sought if additional assets (CSRA) are needed for the support of a "family member" (minor or dependent children, dependent parents, or dependent siblings of the Nursing Home Spouse or of the Community Spouse who are residing with the Community Spouse). For example, an elderly parent or sibling may be residing with the Community Spouse; as a result, a Court Order of Support can increase the assets available to cover the costs associated with supporting that family member through a higher CSRA.

Post-Eligibility Changes to the CSRA

Under the federal statute, after the month in which the Nursing Home Spouse is initially determined to be eligible for Medicaid "no resources of the community spouse shall be deemed available to the institutionalized spouse." Thus, even if the Community Spouse's assets double in value because of good investment performance—or if the Community Spouse wins the lottery or receives an inheritance—those additional assets will not affect the Nursing Home Spouse's Medicaid eligibility and need not be contributed toward the Nursing Home Spouse's care. Although annual redeterminations must be made of the Nursing Home Spouse's assets and income, no such annual redeterminations are necessary or permitted of the Community Spouse's assets.

Sale of Community Spouse's Assets

But what if the Community Spouse sells an excluded asset, such as the home? Under the federal statute just mentioned above, so long as the sale is made after the Nursing

Home Spouse is qualified for Medicaid, it will not affect the Nursing Home Spouse's Medicaid eligibility. The Community Spouse does not have to reinvest the proceeds of the sale; the additional assets are treated just as if the Community Spouse had received an inheritance at that point.

Gift of Community Spouse's Assets

Excluded Assets: If the Community Spouse makes a gift of an excluded asset such as the house to, say, the children, most states will treat this as a disqualifying transfer as to the Nursing Home Spouse as well as the Community Spouse. In other words, the gift could cause the Nursing Home Spouse to be disqualified from Medicaid benefits. As discussed below, the penalty period for a gift normally starts to run on the date of the Medicaid application. But here, because the Nursing Home Spouse is already receiving Medicaid benefits, the Nursing Home Spouse would be disqualified as of the first day of the month the gift was made. Of course, since the Community Spouse was the one who actually made the gift, then should the Community Spouse apply for Medicaid for himself or herself within five years of such gift, the gift will be counted and a penalty period will result in determining Medicaid eligibility of the Community Spouse.

CSRA Assets: If the Community Spouse makes a gift of an asset that was counted as part of the CSRA, on the other hand, no penalty is imposed as to the Nursing Home Spouse, but it is still treated as a potentially penalty-causing gift should the Community Spouse apply for Medicaid for him- or herself within five years of such gift.

Transferring Assets (Gifts)

If you make a gift to anyone other than your spouse, you will be ineligible to receive Medicaid assistance for a certain period of time known as the "penalty period." During this period, even if your assets and income are within the range that would normally allow you to qualify for Medicaid, so long as you are within the penalty period you will be denied Medicaid coverage, barring a hardship exception.

The length of this penalty period depends on the value of your gift. The larger the gift, the longer the penalty period will be. You calculate this penalty period by taking the value of the gifted assets and dividing that value by the average cost of a nursing home in your state. (Every state publishes this "divisor" figure and typically updates it annually, to adjust for inflation.)

It makes no difference how many recipients of the gifts there are. Whether the gift is made to one person or ten, the penalty period is figured the same way: it is based on the total amount of all gifts made during the look-back period. (Do not confuse this rule with the federal law that exempts $13,000 per gift recipient per year. For gift tax purposes it does indeed matter whether the gift is made to one person or ten—but not for Medicaid purposes!)

If you are married, the same penalty period applies whether the gift is made by the person who will be applying for Medicaid or that person's spouse. So having your spouse make the gift instead of you makes no difference.

Example: Let's assume the divisor figure in your state—as determined by your Medicaid department—is $5,000 per month. So if you wrote a check to your daughter for $50,000, you would be ineligible for Medicaid assistance for 10 months: $50,000 gift divided by $5,000 = 10 months.

Now this next point is critical: *There is no limit on the length of the penalty period.*

For example, if you deeded your $350,000 house to your daughter and son today, and if your state divisor figure were $5,000, the penalty period would be 70 months: $350,000 divided by $5,000 = 70 months. I hear you say, "But I thought there is a five-year limit on the penalty?" Five years refers to the look-back period (discussed in the next section), *not* the penalty period. It is important not to confuse the two concepts. Therefore, you could avoid the 70-month penalty simply by not applying for Medicaid until after the 60th month, at which point the gift will be outside the look-back period. So if you applied for Medicaid in month 61, the gift of the house would be ignored for Medicaid eligibility purposes.

Example: On March 1, 2006, John transferred his $350,000 house and $25,000 in cash to his three children. How long must he wait to be eligible for Medicaid benefits? If John applied for Medicaid benefits today and was otherwise eligible, assuming the state divisor figure is $5,000, John would not be covered for 75 months: total amount of gifts ($350,000 + $25,000 = $375,000) divided by $5,000 = 75 months. And if John applied for Medicaid at any time before March 1, 2011, i.e., before the look-back period had expired, he would still be told he was ineligible for Medicaid for another 75 months. Clearly he would be better off not to apply until at least after March 1, 2011; at that point, the two gifts will be ignored since they would be outside of the look-back period.

Result: By waiting until after March 1, 2011 to apply, John's Medicaid coverage could begin as early as March 1, 2011, instead of many months or years later, easily saving his family $350,000 or more.

NOTE: Be sure to check with an experienced elder law attorney in your state if you are about to apply for Medicaid after a look-back period. Different states calculate this differently, and it's better to apply slightly too late than a day too early!

Penalty Start Date: Pre-DRA Gifts

As to any gift made before February 8, 2006, the penalty start date in most states is the first day of the month in which the gift is made (some states start with the following month). In other words, if you wrote a check to your daughter on January 20, 2006, you would normally calculate the penalty period as if you had made the gift on January 1, 2006.

Penalty Start Date: Post-DRA Gifts

As to any gift made on or after February 8, 2006, the penalty start date is the date on which the Medicaid applicant would have been eligible to receive Medicaid coverage but for the imposition of the gift penalty, or, if later, the first day of the month in which the gift is made.

NOTE: The state will use the divisor in effect at the time you apply for Medicaid, not the one in effect on the date of the gift. For example, if you make a gift of $50,000 today when the divisor is $5,000, but you apply for Medicaid four years from now, when the divisor has been increased to $5,500, the penalty will be only 9.1 months, not 10 months.

Gifts by Married Persons

Under the Medicaid rules for married individuals, a penalty can attach to a gift regardless of which spouse actually made the gift or whose money it was. Because the same gift can affect the Medicaid eligibility of both spouses, it seems like the gift is counted twice, but such is not the case. Assuming one of the spouses applies for Medicaid during the look-back period, the full penalty period applies in determining the eligibility of that first spouse; if the other spouse also applies for

Medicaid during the penalty period, then the remaining penalty period is divided equally between the two spouses. Finally, upon the death of one spouse before the expiration of the total number of penalty period months, the total balance will be assigned to the surviving spouse.

Valuing the Gift

The general rule is that the value of a gifted asset is its "fair market value." That means what you could sell it for in a retail sale to the general public in a private party sale.

Automobiles: Look up the Kelly Blue Book value (www.kbb.com). Remember, however, that the one auto is excluded regardless of its value.

Bank Accounts, CDs: Value is based on the amount you would receive if you liquidated the account. So for a CD, only count the amount of interest already credited to your account.

Life Insurance: Only cash value is counted, so ignore the value of term insurance, which has no cash value. Contact the insurance company to obtain a Form 712, which will set forth the current cash value less outstanding loans, if any. That will be the value for Medicaid purposes.

Real Estate: For real estate, you may need to get an appraisal, although often you can rely on the 100 percent value as stated on your most recent real estate tax bill. This is usually spelled out in your state Medicaid regulations.

Stocks, Bonds, Mutual Funds: Since the values of these assets fluctuate daily, obtain the value as of the date of the gift.

Partial Gifts: Occasionally people get the bright idea that if they "sell" some item they own to their children for, say, a dollar, then the entire transaction is no longer a gift. After all, it was a sale, not a gift, right? Unfortunately, that technique doesn't work. In reality, this transaction will be characterized as a part gift, part sale. The amount of compensation received will be subtracted from the fair market value of the asset that was transferred, to arrive at the value of the gift. So if you sell your house to your daughter for $10,000, and the house was appraised at $200,000, then you have made a gift of $190,000 ($200,000 minus $10,000).

Look-Back Period

When a person applies for Medicaid, one of the questions on the intake form will be, "Have you (or your spouse, if married) made any gifts within the past five years?" (Note that a gift by your spouse counts the same as a gift by you.) What the Medicaid workers are looking for are "uncompensated transfers" or "transfers without fair consideration," i.e., gifts, so that they can impose the proper penalty period (discussed above). If the gift was made too long ago, it must be ignored; it would be as if you never made the gift at all, no matter how large a gift it was. How far back the worker can look to see if you made a gift is known as the "look-back period." There are several considerations that apply to gifts, depending on whether they were made "pre-DRA" (i.e., before February 8, 2006) or "post-DRA: (i.e., on or after February 8, 2006) and if they were outright (i.e., given directly to an individual) or made to a trust.

Outright Gifts

When the penalty for gifting was first implemented, the look-back period for outright gifts was 24 months. It was later extended to 30 months, then 36 months, and finally to the current period of 60 months. This means that any gift you made more than five years prior to the date you apply for Medicaid must be ignored. For example, if you transfer your million-dollar house to your children but do not apply for Medicaid until 61 months later, then this very large gift must be ignored and will not count against you. Under the rules effective for post-DRA gifts, there is no benefit to making a gift sooner rather than later unless the person who makes the gift can wait at least a full five years from the date of the gift before applying for Medicaid. That is because the penalty period does not begin to run until the person who made the gift applies for Medicaid.

Example: Sally has only $102,000 of countable assets. Thinking she may need to move into a nursing home in a couple of years, Sally makes a gift of $50,000 on January 1 of next year (Year 1) and another $50,000 on January 1 of the year after that (Year 2). On January 1 of Year 4, Sally has to move into a nursing home. By this time she has no countable assets left (other than her personal exclusion of $2,000), so ordinarily she would have qualified for Medicaid. However, since she made gifts within the past five years of her application date, the two $50,000 gifts must be added together and treated as if she made the gifts on the day she applied for Medicaid. So her $100,000 of total gifts will now cause her to be disqualified for a period equal to $100,000 divided by $5,000 (assuming that's the state penalty divisor figure) = 20 months. If Sally waits until January 1 of Year 6 to apply for Medicaid, only the second gift of $50,000 will count against her, since the first gift is now more than five years old. Finally, if Sally instead waits until January 1 of Year 7, then she will immediately qualify for Medicaid, because more than five years have passed since the date of her last gift.

DRA Transition Rules

Outright gifts made on or after February 8, 2006, are subject to the new five-year look-back rule. Since the old rule still applies as to any gifts made prior to this date, this change really had no effect until more than three years had gone by, i.e., after February 8, 2009. At that point, the look-back period as to outright gifts will be extended one month for each month that passes. In other words, for an application made on December 8, 2009, the look-back period for outright gifts will be three years, 10 months (i.e., only back to February 8, 2006), and not five years. The Medicaid workers cannot go back further than that, because any gifts made before February 8, 2006, were only subject to a 36-month look-back period, and we're already beyond that at this point in time.

Estate Recovery

Upon the death of any individual who was covered by Medicaid while institutionalized (or a non-institutionalized Medicaid recipient who was at least age 55 at the time of receiving benefits), the state must seek to recover all of the expenditures it made on behalf of the now-deceased Medicaid recipient for nursing home costs, medical costs (hospital and prescription drugs) while in the nursing home, Medicare premiums and co-payments during this time, and HCBS payments. Since this recovery is not made until after the death of the recipient, it is known as "estate recovery."

In essence, while you thought you had qualified for a government benefit, all you've really received is an interest-free loan! And upon your death, the government wants its loan paid back.

Prior to 1993, such estate recovery was optional—a state could implement it or not. However, in that year a new federal law was passed (known as OBRA '93) that mandated that every state must seek estate recovery from its Medicaid-receiving residents following their deaths. While some states managed to delay implementation of this federally mandated law until just recently, by now every state finally has a recovery statute in place.

This is an odd situation. If you qualified for Medicaid, then you're essentially broke so you wouldn't have money to repay the state. If your family member died owning nothing, then indeed the state is out of luck. It can't go after the kids' money. It can't go after a surviving Community Spouse's money. There must be some assets that the nursing home resident had a legal interest in at the time of death, in order for the state to be repaid. That legal interest is defined as the "estate" of the deceased Medicaid recipient. However, the definition of "estate" varies from state to state, thereby affecting what assets the particular state can recover against.

Definition of "Estate"

All states must seek recovery at least from the "probate estate" of the Medicaid recipient. This is typically defined to include only assets that would pass by will. Such definition includes assets titled in the sole name of the decedent, but excludes assets that pass by beneficiary designation (such as a life insurance policy, annuity, IRA, 401(k), or similar plan payable to someone other than the insured's estate); POD (pay on death) bank accounts; TOD (transfer on death) stock certificates or brokerage accounts; trust property; joint bank accounts; and jointly owned real estate or other property that passes by operation of law automatically to the surviving owner(s) by right of survivorship.

Expanded Definition of "Estate"

Under the federal law, any state may adopt an expanded definition of "estate," to include any one or more of the following: assets conveyed to a survivor, heir or assign of the deceased individual through joint tenancy, tenancy in common, survivorship, life estate, living trust, or other arrangement (such as an annuity). In other words, the definition of "estate" could include virtually any asset in which the deceased nursing home resident had any legal interest the moment before death. Currently, only 13 states actually limit estate recovery to probate assets, with the other states adopting various degrees of the maximum permitted by federal law. It is important that you know exactly what is and what is not subject to estate recovery in your particular state, so that you may plan accordingly.

Planning for Change

Unfortunately, even if you reside in a state that does not currently use an expanded definition of "estate," there is no guarantee that it may not do so at some time in the near future. Worse, a recent case held that there is no "grandfathering" for Medicaid recipients when the law changes midway through their nursing home stay. Whatever law is in effect upon the death of a Medicaid recipient will apply, even if that means that assets that were not subject to recovery earlier in the recipient's nursing home stay may be subject to recovery at the time of his or her death. This is another reason for only working with an elder law attorney who not only keeps up with legislation that may be introduced in your state affecting estate recovery, but who is also aware of trends in other states that may affect future legislation in your state. Of course, there is always the possibility that laws may change, and no attorney has a crystal ball, but you increase your odds of doing the best possible planning by working with a "plugged-in" and savvy elder law attorney.

There are some exceptions that prevent estate recovery. If you were under age 55 at the time you received Medicaid benefits, other than nursing home care, you will be exempt from estate recovery for the amount of those benefits. And no recovery may be made against your estate until after the death of whichever of the following may survive you:

- your spouse
- a child of yours who is under age 21
- a dependent of yours who is blind or totally and permanently disabled, as defined under the Social Security regulations

Unlike the Tax Equity and Fiscal Responsibility Act of 1982 (TEFRA) lien rules discussed below, it is not necessary that these individuals be living in your home for these exceptions to apply.

There will also be no recovery made against your home (i.e., it will not have to be sold to pay back the state) if:

1. a sibling of yours was living in the house for at least one year immediately prior to the date you were admitted to the nursing home and has continuously lived in the house since then, or
2. there is a son or daughter (of any age) of yours who was living in the house for at least two years immediately prior to the date you were

admitted to the nursing home, and has continuously lived in the house since then, and who provided care to you prior to your entering the nursing home which permitted you to delay entering the nursing home.

If all else fails, there's an exception to estate recovery if such recovery would work an "undue hardship" on the surviving family members. One example would be where the excluded asset is a working farm, and a forced sale of that farm would throw surviving family members out of work.

Timing of the Recovery Claim

Technically, the federal law states that recovery can be made "only after the death of the individual's surviving spouse." So if, for example, the surviving spouse dies a month after the Medicaid recipient, a state could file a claim for recovery at that time. Many states have taken a more liberal reading of this, and for so long as there is a surviving spouse no recovery will be made, no matter how long the surviving spouse lives. You'll need to check your own state's laws to find out which rule applies to your situation.

Even in states where recovery may be made after the surviving spouse's death, there is, typically, an additional limitation that applies to all claims against an estate: all states have a statute of limitations that bars claims against an estate that are made more than a certain number of months after the death. In many states, that limit is one year. So, in a state with such a law, if the surviving spouse dies more than a year after the Medicaid recipient spouse, it will be too late for the state Medicaid recovery unit to file its claim for estate recovery. Some states have gotten around this limitation by filing the claim within the limitations period, but delaying recovery until after the death of the surviving spouse.

If a state can only file a claim when there is no child under age 21, can it wait until the child attains age 21 and then file its recovery claim? Once again, this must happen within the statute of limitations period, assuming there's not a blanket exemption if there's a surviving child under age 21.

Procedure and Time Limit

If recovery is limited to the "probate estate," then the state must file a timely claim against the estate, just as any other creditor of the decedent must do. Many states limit this time period to file a claim to one year after the date of death. If the state files a claim for estate recovery too late, it is out of luck.

If a lien was filed against the house, however, the state may have a longer time in which to satisfy its claim (see "Liens"). Exactly how much longer depends on the lien law of your state. You would need to check with an elder law attorney in your state, but be prepared for the attorney not knowing the answer right off the bat, since this is an unsettled question in many states.

Sometimes the family of a deceased Medicaid recipient will attempt the "lay low" approach, not opening a probate estate and hoping that the limitations period will expire before the state files its claim. If that happens, then the family will indeed "win," since at that point it will be too late for the state to collect its money from the estate. However, many states have now implemented procedures for being notified of the death of anyone in a nursing home who was a Medicaid recipient, and if probate of the estate is not opened by the family within 30 days, the state itself—as a creditor—may petition the court to open the estate, and then file its claim for estate recovery.

Waivers

In certain limited circumstances, the state must refrain from seeking recovery against the estate if it would result in undue hardship. For example, a disabled family member may be living in the deceased Medicaid recipient's home, and it would be deemed a hardship if there were a forced sale of the house, rendering the family member homeless.

In addition, a state may waive recovery if it is not cost-effective, i.e., the value of the house (or the amount to be recovered) is small in relation to the administrative cost of seeking recovery.

Married Couples' Issues

In planning for estate recovery for a married couple, one must consider the possibility that either spouse may be the survivor.

If the Nursing Home Spouse Dies First: Following the death of the Nursing Home Spouse, the state is limited to recovering assets in which the Nursing Home Spouse had a legal interest at the time of death. However, if there is a surviving spouse, federal law bars the state from filing for estate recovery until after the surviving spouse dies. The states are divided among those that completely waive estate recovery if there is a surviving spouse, those that merely defer enforcement of the claim until the later death of the spouse, and those that use a combination approach. In any event, the state can never go after assets that were always owned solely by the surviving Community Spouse.

As a general rule, the state can only go after assets in the deceased Nursing Home Spouse's "estate" by filing a claim against that estate. Under the expanded definition of "estate" (see page 109), however, assets that pass to someone else immediately upon the death of the Nursing Home Spouse may still be subject to recovery.

How can the state identify those interests? A few states have begun to apply a "tracing" approach, whereby assets that once belonged to the Nursing Home Spouse and that passed into the name of the Community Spouse at the death of the Nursing Home Spouse (whether by will, right of survivorship, etc.) can be reached by the estate recovery rules.

However, only the highest court of one state (North Dakota, 2000) has interpreted federal law to allow claims against the estate of the surviving Community Spouse for assets that were transferred to that spouse by the Nursing Home Spouse before the death of the Nursing Home Spouse. If the state can prove the Nursing Home Spouse once held an interest in some part of the surviving Community Spouse's estate, those assets can be subject to estate recovery and the state can file a claim against the Community Spouse's estate. Luckily for people living in the other 49 states that this interpretation doesn't currently apply to them!

If the Community Spouse Dies First: If the Community Spouse predeceases the Nursing Home Spouse, the big issue is what happens to the assets owned by the Community Spouse upon his or her death. The last thing you want to have happen is for the assets to pass to the surviving spouse, who is in the nursing home on Medicaid. If that happens, the Nursing Home Spouse will be immediately disqualified from receiving Medicaid, by virtue of being "over resourced," and any of those inherited assets still in the surviving spouse's name at his or her death will be subject to estate recovery. Accordingly, this possibility must be carefully planned for, because you never know which spouse may die first. (See detailed discussion beginning on page 114.)

Avoiding Estate Recovery

As discussed above, merely qualifying for Medicaid is not enough if, upon the Medicaid recipient's death, the state can file a claim against the property of the deceased recipient, demanding to be repaid every dime of benefits it paid out on behalf of the recipient. However, there are some planning techniques that you can implement to minimize or eliminate the state's right of recovery.

Liens: To prevent Medicaid recipients from disposing of their assets prior to death, thereby avoiding the state's attempt at estate recovery, states are permitted to file "liens" against certain property of a Medicaid recipient.

A lien against your home is a recorded document filed by your creditor that prohibits the sale of your home without first satisfying the existing debt. It is similar to a mortgage, which prohibits you from selling your house without first paying off the bank. In the Medicaid context, it is filed by the state to guarantee repayment of all the money it will pay out for your care while you are on the Medicaid program.

Under the Tax Equity and Fiscal Responsibility Act of 1982 (known as "TEFRA"), states have the option of imposing liens to ensure repayment of their Medicaid expenditures. Thus, the state you live in may or may not impose liens.

Following notice and opportunity for a hearing, a lien may be placed on the home of the Medicaid recipient once it is established that the recipient is not expected to return to his or her home. This should not be confused with the continued exclusion of the home. No matter how unlikely it may be that the Medicaid recipient will ever return home, so long as the "intent to return home" is maintained, your home is not counted as a financial resource. In other words, the state can determine that you are both unlikely ever to return to your home for TEFRA lien purposes and likely to return home for Medicaid eligibility purposes!

The lien may be filed, no matter how old you are, so long as you are receiving Medicaid for nursing home or home and community based services (HCBS). Recovery may only be made after the death of the Medicaid recipient or, if sooner, upon the sale of the home.

Exceptions: The lien may not be imposed at the time any of the following are lawfully residing in your home:

- your spouse
- a child of yours who is under age 21

- a child of yours who is permanently blind or disabled, as defined under the Social Security regulations
- a brother or sister of yours who has an equity interest in your house and who has lived there at least one year prior to your entering the nursing home

The lien may not be enforced if any of the following are lawfully residing in your home and have been lawfully residing in your home since the date you entered the nursing home: a child of yours who lived there at least two years prior to your entering the nursing home and whose care allowed you to delay your going there; or a brother or sister of yours (who may or may not have an equity interest in your house) who has lived there at least one year prior to your entering the nursing home.

Finally, the lien must be removed if you leave the nursing home and actually move back home.

NOTE: For planning techniques, case studies, tables showing the applicable figures for each of the 50 states, and additional examples and information regarding the Medicaid program as it relates to nursing home payments, see *Medicaid Secrets* by K. Gabriel Heiser, J.D., available online at www.MedicaidSecrets.com.

This chapter covers the important information about Medicaid and other government programs. But as you have seen, this is a complicated subject. I urge you to review this chapter carefully and seek guidance from an experienced elder care attorney or financial advisor if you're facing any of these decisions for yourself or a loved one.

What if you run out of money and need long term care?
"5 Ways to Finance Retirement until Age 100" is available to download at:
http://krismillermoneymaestro.com/finance-retirement
Learn more at: http://ReadyForPREtirement.com

"Create a definite plan for carrying out your desire and begin at once, whether you are ready or not, to put this plan into action."
— **Napoleon Hill**

Chapter 5

FINANCIAL LEGACY AND THE EXCELLENT PRETIREMENT CHOICE

"Only those who risk going too far can possibly find out how far they can go."
— **T. S. Eliot**

Insurance and annuity expert Karlan Tucker, CEO, Tucker Advisory Group, is a powerful spokesperson for the benefits of annuities—specifically, the Fixed Index Annuity (FIA). I am featuring his article "No Risk, Just Reward" (for which he has graciously given me permission) to explain how an FIA works and its benefits, which include:

- Your principal is safe, along with your previously captured gains.
- You don't have to accept a modest return in exchange for no risk.

- Company expenses are paid from a "spread" of gains from conservative investments.
- You have a choice of indices in which to participate.
- Because it's a tax-deferred vehicle, you capture gains without triggering a taxable event.
- FIAs typically allow an annual 10 percent withdrawal without any fees or penalties.
- FIAs have no required fees, loads, or commissions taken from your growing principal (agent compensation comes out of company's spread, not account values).
- FIAs offer income features that allow for a minimum growth during the deferral phase of up to 8 percent compounded annually for a maximum of 20 years.
- Any principal remaining in your account at death is inheritable by your beneficiaries, allowing you to generate a sustainable income for life because the company uses an annual fee of .45 to .65 basis points to reinsure the risk of your living longer than life expectancy tables predict.
- FIAs can be appropriate for both qualified—IRAs, 401(k)s 403(b)s—and non-qualified dollars.
- You have peace of mind knowing you won't lose your life savings.

No Risk, Just Reward

Remember back to the days when the financial advice you heard over and over again was to take a risk? In investments, the stock market, even savings accounts, if you wanted to reap the rewards, you had to risk your money. That is no longer true. A Fixed Index Annuity (FIA) offers the balance of reward but without the market risk! It's a product perfect for today's volatile markets.

It works like this: when the opportunity of a rising market occurs, the FIA captures it for life. But when the markets slide into a downturn, this product protects our principal and all previously captured gains.

When investing, a lot of the fun comes from not knowing what your reward will be. The FIA holds onto that unknown factor, while assuring you that there won't be any losses. This provides a peace of mind not available when putting your money in a stock or mutual fund, where there's a chance of a reward, but just as much of a chance at a loss.

As of 2007, over $115 billion was being placed in FIAs, ensuring their popularity as a tool for protecting and growing nest eggs.

Previously, people had two choices: they could be investors or savers. The investor was willing to risk principal in the stock market for the opportunity of better gain. The saver accepted a modest return in exchange for less risk. The FIA filled the gaping hole between the two, by protecting the principal by placing it in a conservative bond portfolio that is usually anchored in U.S. government treasuries.

"To get a better yield without taking significant credit risk," says Karlan Tucker, CEO, Tucker Advisory Group, "the balance of the portfolio is then typically invested in the highest quality corporate bonds with a very small amount—typically less than 10 percent—in either higher-yielding bonds or commercial mortgages. The purpose of the bond portfolio is to provide a safe place to park the principal; and it accomplishes this very effectively, as evidenced by the fact that no owner of an FIA has ever lost any principal or interest due to either the failure of the issuing financial entity or market risk."

The financial entity then takes a "spread" from the gross yield of the bonds, producing the net yield. The insurance company uses the spread to pay its expenses and garner a profit for itself and its shareholders.

The net yield can then be either given to the FIA owner or used to option in to their chosen index from the S&P 500 to Dow Jones to bond or European indices.

FIAs use only the renewable resource of yield to purchase an option that controls a position in an index equal to the size of their principal. A $100,000 investment in an FIA means the option purchased would have a $100,000 value. So the principal is represented in the market without actually putting it there. On your anniversary date, your option captures a return. That return is put into a conservative bond portfolio for safekeeping. It won't be lost to a future market's volatility. And your gain is tax-free since the FIA is a tax-deferred product.

A 10 percent withdrawal without fees or penalties is allowed annually. Today's FIAs income features allow a minimum growth during the deferral phase of up to 8 percent compounded annually for a maximum of 20 years. Some offer additional potential for annually increasing income during the distribution phase. This happens when the FIA is linked to the fixed account or an index with an income increase equal to the chosen strategy's performance.

Any remaining principal in your account at death is inheritable by your beneficiaries. The only fees associated with an FIA are the annual fees between .45 and .65 basis points.

FIAs eliminate the emotion from investing because you never have to worry about a market loss. Your ability to generate a sustainable income for life is dramatically enhanced since it reinsures the risk of your living longer than life expectancy tables predict.

FIAs can be appropriate for both qualified—IRAs, 401(k)s, 403(b)s—and non-qualified—already taxed—dollars.

The FIA is a highly recommended product designed to protect and grow your nest egg by providing no market risk, just reward. It is really no wonder that FIA owners gladly trade some of the up for none of the down.

The Top Three Myths of Financial Planning

Most people who have a 401(k) or an IRA have little idea of where their money is invested. When you ask them, "Where's your retirement money?" they reply, "At the bank" or "With my broker." No wonder so many people are financially unprepared for retirement.

The fact is that if you want to be financially secure in your golden years, you must take control of your investments… today! Handing over your money to a broker and hoping someone else will look out for you is a recipe for disaster. Imagine saving and investing for 40-plus years, only to find out at age 65 or 70 that you don't have enough money to retire. It's a common scenario that happens every day.

But with so much financial planning information available, why are so many people still financially unprepared for retirement? Because there are certain financial planning myths that simply won't go away. And the more you believe the myths, the more of a struggle your retirement will be. Let's clear up these myths once and for all so you can take charge of your financial future and be prepared for retirement.

Myth #1: You have to put your money at risk in order to make a decent return.

Most 401(k)s and IRAs are invested in the stock market. But the stock market is the riskiest place to put your money. You've likely heard "market experts" say that now is a good time to invest in the stock market. Really? A broken watch tells the right time twice a day, but that's no reason to wear one. According to the experts, stocks, on average provide about 10 percent return annually. But this assumption goes back to the 1800s and no longer applies in the 21st century. Today, your typical annual return from investing in the stock market is closer to 5 percent.

Likewise, you've likely heard people say, "Our economists are forecasting…." Ask your broker if the firm's economists predicted the most recent recession, and if so, when? Warren Buffett once said that forecasters make fortunetellers look good. If you want to earn higher returns, most brokers tell you that you have to take more risk. This must come as a surprise to Mr. Buffett, who prefers investing in boring blue chip industries.

Here's the truth: there's no reason for your money to be at risk. You can make money with safer investments, such as fixed index annuities, which are like a savings account with an insurance company. In fact, even during the Great Depression, not one person lost money with a fixed index annuity. They're safe, they have liquidity, and they offer better rates than most other products.

So why hasn't your broker told you about these less risky options? See Myth #2.

Myth #2: Your broker only makes money when you do.

It's nice to think that your broker only cares about you and your financial future, but that's not 100 percent true. While your broker likely does want the best for you, here's what usually happens when you let him or her invest your money. Your broker buys shares of stocks and mutual funds. The market can then go in one of three directions: up, down, or stagnant. Wall Street can't control the market, and neither can your broker.

Here's the important point: brokers don't make money when you do. Sure, they'd like you to make money, but they actually make their money by *managing* your money. They make money when the market goes down; they make money when the market goes up; they make money when the market is flat. In other words, they always win. Their clients, however (and that would be you), only win in one of those three directions. Brokers win in all three directions.

Since your broker makes money by managing your money (by moving your money from fund to fund and by buying and selling shares of stocks), why would he or she want to have you invest in something boring, like the fixed index annuity mentioned before—especially since the less risky products typically offer brokers a one-time commission and nothing more? In contrast, there are big commissions in stock market investing. Every time your broker buys or sells stocks for you, not only do they charge you a fee (see Myth #3), but they also get a commission. Knowing this, whom do you think most brokers are really looking out for?

Myth #3: Maintaining a stock portfolio is very inexpensive.

Even though you may be putting money into your retirement account on a regular basis, hidden fees may be slowly draining your account. The disclosed fees are simple to find; look at the expense ratio, which is found in the prospectus. These fees are commonly referred to as "management fees."

Administration fees are in addition to the management fees and are much harder to find. At first, you may think that a small fee here and a nominal fee there is no big deal. After all, how much could these administration fees possibly be? Well, consider this: according to the U.S. Department of Labor 401(k) fee website, "Assume you are an employee with 35 years until retirement and a current 401(k) account balance of $25,000. If returns on investments in your account over the next 35 years average 7 percent and fees and expenses reduce your average returns by 0.5 percent, your account balance will grow to $227,000 at retirement, even if there are no further contributions to your account. If fees and expenses are 1.5 percent, however, your account balance will grow to only $163,000. The 1 percent difference in fees and expenses would reduce your account balance at retirement by 28 percent." That's a huge fee!

Therefore, be sure to look for and ask your broker about the following fees:

- plan administration fees
- investment fees
- individual service fees

Knowing the truth about hidden fees and taking action to avoid them can add thousands of dollars to your retirement savings.

Plan Your Future Today

Whether you plan to retire today or in another 30 years, you need to take control of your retirement accounts right away. Understanding how your money is invested and making sure it's working for you in the most efficient way will give you both peace of mind and future security. By dispelling the key myths of financial planning and investing a little time and energy creating your future financial plan, you can rest assured that your retirement years will be pleasurable... and prosperous.

SUMMARY AND PLAN OF ACTION

I hope that this book has taught you how important it is for you to start making plans earlier to ensure you have assets to enjoy your time, both before and during retirement. I've provided you with the tools to get you started in PREtirement. Whether you implement some of the strategies I recommend on your own or by consulting your own planner is your choice. But my last words on that: you shouldn't hesitate. Take the time now—while you have it—to act on these ideas, complete the forms and discuss your plans with your loved ones. PREpare for the unexpected now, follow up on the PREtirement recommendations and have the Estate of Mind that comes from securing your own financial future.

Learn more at: http://ReadyForPREtirement.com.

ABOUT KRIS MILLER, CHFEB, CSA, LDA

As a PREtirement and living trust expert and national speaker, Kris Miller assists people in developing complete estate packages. Her practice focuses on helping seniors reduce their tax liabilities, make safe investments, and protect their savings from probate, nursing home spend-down, and the seizure of assets to pay medical debts.

For more than 20 years, Miller has given PREtirement workshops and keynotes to educate people and organizations about wise money management. In 2010, she was nominated Woman of the Year and Best Customer Service by the Hemet, CA, Chamber of Commerce.

Kris is a Certified Senior Advisor, a professional who has knowledge about aging and the important health, financial, and social issues that affect the majority of PREtirees. She is also a Chartered Federal Employee Benefits Consultant. ChFEBCs are financial professionals who are required to stay up to date on the ever-changing federal government benefits programs and maintain extensive knowledge about FERS, CSRS, Special Provisions (LEO, FF, ATC, CBPO).

In addition to her estate planning practice, Kris owns Trusts Unlimited and The Living Trust Institute, a document preparation service for Revocable Living Trusts.

A talented singer/songwriter, Kris shares wisdom and comfort with others through her inspirational gospel music. Since stepping into the professional music sphere in 2007, she has won several prestigious songwriting awards, including being named Songwriter of the Year in three categories by the National American Country Music Awards in 2010, and being nominated in 2010 and in 2011 as Songwriter of the Year by Inspirational Country Music Awards. Her first CD, "Live and Well," released in 2007, was entered into the Grammy process, as was her latest, "The Journey Home."

She had her first number one hit in Europe in 2010 and in the U.S. in 2009.

This is why they call Kris Miller the "Money Maestro." She harmonizes people's finances and keeps them singing "in tune" financially—with safety, protection and growth.

To invite Kris Miller to speak before your group, contact her:

Telephone: 951 926-4158 and 951 926-4538
kris@ReadyForPREtirement.com
www.ReadyForPREtirement.com
www.KrisMillerMoneyMaestro.com
www.KrisMillerSpeaker.com

AN INVITATION FROM
KRIS MILLER

I want to hear from *You!*

I meant what I said in the author's notes: if you have suggestions or comments about the book, please email me with your suggestions or your own experiences. With your permission, I will share these examples with others on my blogs and web sites.

Best wishes and many blessings—

Kris Miller

kris@ReadyForPREtirement.com

www.ReadyForPREtirement.com

Please go to my site and sign up for our quarterly report so you can receive the latest information about new laws and regulations, along with the headline stories that may affect your plans for retirement.

APPENDIX CONTENTS

A   Organization of Documents

B   Revocable Living Trusts

C   Checklist of Activities After a Death

D   Documents Checklist

E   Personal Information and Funeral Plans

F   Assets & Possessions

G   Family Medical Information

Appendix A

ORGANIZATION OF DOCUMENTS

Below is a list of documents that you should have organized, accessible, and protected from fire or theft. You may wish to place them all together in a fireproof home safe or in a safety deposit box at a financial institution.

Name _____

Social Security Number _____ Date Completed _____

Primary Doctor _____ Telephone _____

Lawyer _____ Telephone _____

Accountant_____ Telephone _____

Power of Attorney _____ Telephone _____

Health Care Agent _____ Telephone _____

Investment Broker _____ Telephone _____

Clergy _____ Telephone _____

Emergency Contact _____ Telephone _____

Emergency Contact _____ Telephone _____

Personal Information: Where is it kept?

Birth Certificate _____

Marriage Certificate _____

Divorce Papers _____

Military Records_____

    Branch of Service _____

    Military ID # _____

    Dates of Service_____

Organ Donor Card _____

Passport / Citizenship Papers _____

Will _____

Trusts _____

Safety Deposit Box_____

    Number _____Location of keys_____

Insurance Information: Where is it kept?

Automobile _____

Disability _____

Homeowners _____

Life_____

Long Term Care _____

Health _____

Other _____

Financial Information: Where is it kept?

Automobile Title/Registration _____

Bank Statements_____

Bonds/CDs _____

Bank Account # (Checking) _____

Bank Account # (Saving) _____

Bank Account # (Money Market) _____

401(k) Account _____

IRA Account _____

Mortgage Information _____

Outstanding Loans_____

Property Deeds/Title _____

Stock Certificates _____

Income Tax Records _____

Pension Records _____

Medical Information: Where is it kept?

Advance Directives _____

Do Not Resuscitate Papers _____

Health Care Power of Attorney _____ Telephone _____

Living Will_____

Final Wishes: Where is it kept?

Burial Arrangements_____

Cemetery Information _____

Funeral Home _____

Appendix B

REVOCABLE LIVING TRUSTS

TRUST UNLIMITED
REVOCABLE LIVING TRUSTS PREPARATION

KRIS MILLER 951.926.4158

REFERRAL _____ DATE_____ COSTS $ _____

FILE # _____

INTAKE DATE_____ BY _____

TYPE OF TRUST _____

RECEIPT # _____ AMT. CK. $ _____

ADDRESS _____

PHONE: (   ) _____

==

1. NAME (Spouse/Partner 1/Single Individual) _____

2. Spouse/Partner 2 _____

SS# _____ - _____ - _____   SS# _____ - _____ - _____

3. NAME OF TRUST " THE _____ TRUST"

4. COUNTY OF RESIDENCE _____ 5. STATE _____

6. COUNTY DOCS. EXECUTED _____ 7. STATE _____

8. CITY _____

9. SUCCESSOR TRUSTEE _____

RELATIONSHIP _____

ALTERNATE _____

RELATIONSHIP _____

10. EXECUTOR OF WILL (Spouse/Partner 1/Individual) _____

ALTERNATE _____

11. EXECUTOR OF WILL (Spouse/Partner 2) _____

ALTERNATE _____

12. GUARDIAN OF MINOR CHILDREN _____

ALTERNATE _____

13. POWER OF ATTORNEY (Spouse/Partner 1/Individual) _____

ALTERNATE _____

14. POWER OF ATTORNEY (Spouse/Partner 2)_____

ALTERNATE _____

15. POWER OF ATT. HEALTH (Spouse/Partner 1/Individual) _____

ALTERNATE _____

16. POWER OF ATT. HEALTH (Spouse/Partner 2)_____

ALTERNATE _____

17. SPECIAL NEEDS (Spouse/Partner 1/Individual) (a)_____ (b)_____

SPECIAL NEEDS (Spouse/Partner 2) (a)_____ (b)_____

18. NOTES _____

19 AGE DISTRIBUTION TO FINAL BENEFICIARIES _____

20. PERCENTAGE OR FRACTIONAL SHARE OF EACH BENEFICIARY

_____

_____

_____

21. THE SHARE OF A DECEASED BENEFICIARY SHALL BE DISTRIBUTED TO:

_____

_____

_____

22. NAMES OF ALL CHILDREN (SPOUSE/PARTNER 1/INDIVIDUAL)

_____

_____

_____

23. NAMES OF ALL CHILDREN (SPOUSE/PARTNER 2)

_____

_____

_____

DECEASED _____ ISSUE _____

DECEASED _____ ISSUE _____

24. SPECIAL GIFTS OF TRUST PROPERTY

_____

25. TOTAL NUMBER OF DEED(S) _____ A.P. # _____

MY ESTATE: $_____IN ASSETS AND/OR

$_____IN REAL ESTATE

(In California, any estate worth over $100,000 in assets or $20,000 in real estate goes to probate. Please check the amounts in the state where you live.)

THE ABOVEMENTIONED PROVISIONS ARE CORRECT AND IN ACCORDANCE WITH MY/OUR UNDERSTANDING AND I/WE ASK THAT THEY BE INCLUDED IN MY/OUR REVOCABLE LIVING TRUST.

© Kris Miller

Appendix C

CHECKLIST OF ACTIVITIES AFTER A DEATH

Funeral Arrangements:

____ Review decedent's funeral and burial instructions, if any.

____ Review decedent's desires concerning gifts of body or body parts.

____ Call a mortuary and make funeral and burial arrangements.

____ Notify immediate family, friends and employer.

____ Collect information for the obituary and call the newspaper.

Immediate Care of Decedent's Property:

____ Ensure that decedent's home is secure and notify landlord.

____ Remove valuables and important documents to a safe place.

____Contact utility companies to discontinue services, including forwarding mail.

____ Check to ensure that insurance coverage will continue for a period of time.

Administration of the Estate:

____ Contact decedent's estate planning attorney.

____Request at least five certified copies of the Death Certificate from the mortuary.

____ Assemble important documents (living trusts, bankbooks, stock certificates, real estate deeds, insurance policies, etc.).

_____ Prepare summary of decedent's assets and liabilities, including fair values.

_____ Examine the decedent's checkbooks, tax returns and other financial records.

_____Arrange to have any appreciated assets valued (e.g., stocks, bonds, real estate).

_____ Contact insurance companies to make claims for any death insurance.

_____ Contact Social Security for benefits.

_____ Contact the Veterans Administration for benefits, if appropriate.

_____ Contact the decedent's employer and, if appropriate, union or professional groups, to determine possible benefits.

_____ Prepare a list of obligations (e.g., outstanding credit card bills).

_____ Verify the existence of possible death insurance to pay any balances.

_____ Cancel all credit cards held in decedent's name.

_____ Ensure all vehicles and property of the estate are properly insured.

_____ When all liabilities, debts, and assets are known and valued, pay all obligations.

_____ Under the direction of the estate planning attorney, change title of deceased's assets to successor trustee or successor beneficiary, as appropriate. Your attorney assists in making the transfers of real estate and supervises the transfer of all other assets.

_____ Contact the accountant. Allocate assets to A-B or A-B-C Trust, as appropriate.

_____Obtain tax identification numbers for B and C Trusts.

_____ If decedent's net estate is $600,000 or more, have accountant file a federal Estate Tax Return, Form 706, and any required state Estate Returns. Ensure that the returns are filed on time. (Significant penalties and interest are charged for late returns.)

_____ Prepare applicable state/federal income tax returns for tax year the decedent died.

Appendix D

DOCUMENTS CHECKLIST

Gather your official, financial, and legal documents and let your spouse, key family member(s), personal representative, or executor know where they are located for easy access/retrieval.

Documents	Physical Location of Originals (and/or name of hard drive location of computer file)	Location of copies (if applicable) or names of people who have copies with date given
5 Wishes Document (if applicable— see www.agingwithdignity.org)		
"Family Organizer" manual		
Automobile Titles		
Birth Certificates or Adoption Papers		
Business Agreements		
Business or Partnership Agreements		
Citizenship Papers		
Death Certificates		
Debt/Loan Certificates		
Deeds		
Disability Insurance Policies		
Divorce/Separation Papers (if applicable)		
Employee Life Insurance Policies		
Financial Account Numbers		
Financial/Bank/Inv. Statements		
Funeral Instructions		
Home & Vehicle Insurance Policies		

Leases		
Life Insurance Policies		
Marriage Certificates		
Medical Power of Attorney		
Memos/Instructions about distribution of personal, sentimental, or heirloom possessions		
Military Discharge Papers		
Mortgages		
Partnerships		
Passports		
Past Income Tax Returns		
Personal address book		
Personal Financial Statement		
Power of Attorney		
Prepaid Funeral Arrangements		
Recreational Vehicle/Equip Titles		
Retirement/Pension Benefits		
Social Security Cards & Benefits*		
Stock Certificates/Bonds		
Wills/Trusts/Estate Plans		
Other:		
Other:		

Safe Deposit Box Info (if applicable):

Physical Location: _____

Box Number: _____

Location of keys: _____

Name of Financial Institution: _____

Phone Number: _____

Address: _____

*Note about Social Security Benefits. The SS phone number is 1-800-772-1213. To claim SS death benefits after the death of a spouse, go to your local Social Security office and bring with you your spouse's death certificate, Social Security card, birth certificate, marriage certificate/license, and the birth certificates for each child.

From *Family Organizer* (www.familyorganizer.org)
by Dr. Brian Kluth and used with permission.

Appendix E

PERSONAL INFORMATION
AND FUNERAL PLANS

Use additional paper if necessary.

Full Name _____

Social Security Number _____

Date of Birth (*DOB*) _____ Place of Birth_____

Driver's License State/Number _____

Full Name of Father_____

Father's Birthplace _____ Father's DOB _____

Full Name of Mother _____

Mother's Birthplace _____ Mother's DOB _____

Siblings and their current location

_____

_____

_____

_____

If married, Wedding Date_____

Spouse's Maiden Name _____ DOB _____

Child #1 Name_____

DOB_____Soc Sec # _____Spouse _____

Child #2 Name_____

DOB_____Soc Sec # _____Spouse _____

Child #3 Name_____

DOB_____Soc Sec # _____Spouse _____

Child #4 Name_____

DOB_____Soc Sec # _____Spouse _____

Occupations/Position/Title/Years _____

Employers/Years _____

Do you have any life insurance with an Accidental Death Benefit (*which pays extra if you died accidentally*)? _____

Grade School(s), Middle School/Jr. Highs/Cities_____

High School(s)/City/Year Graduated _____

College(s)/Universities/Years/Cities/Degrees/Majors _____

Places lived in/years _____

Military from _____to _____ in the (branch) _____

Rank _____ Serial # _____ Discharge Date _____

Places served in Military _____

Churches Attended/Cities/Years _____

Professional Groups, Civic, Clubs, Lodges, Associations _____

_____

Closest friends_____

_____

FUNERAL PLANNING: Provide instructions, notes, name(s), addresses, phone numbers, emails, etc.

Church/City _____ Phone _____

Funeral Home/City_____

If prepaid, account # _____ Phone _____

Cemetery/City _____

If purchased, what row #_____Lot # _____Block #_____ Section #_____

Casket or Urn Company _____

If prepaid, account # _____ Phone _____

Preferred Clergy _____

Meal after funeral?_____ Where? _____

Memorial Service (*in another city?*)_____

Obituaries (what cities?) _____

Preferred Pallbearers _____

Flowers? _____Or Memorials to?_____

Special Songs Requested _____

Special Scriptures _____

Special Poems or Stories _____

Preferred Singer/s _____

Preferred Instrumentalist/s _____

Preferred Speaker/s _____

Should gospel (*and/or testimony*) be shared?_____

Invitation for salvation given? _____

Instructions for choosing casket or urn _____

Clothing or jewelry desires _____

Grave marker choice _____

Location of will, policies, etc. _____

Viewing choice: ☐ Public Viewing ☐ Private family viewing only ☐ No viewing

Burial/Cremation choice: ☐ Casket followed by burial ☐ Casket followed by cremation
☐ Cremation

If casket, open or closed? _____

If cremated, what to do with ashes? _____

Items for the memorial table _____

Location of photos (*computer files?*) _____

Other _____

_____

_____

_____

_____

From *Family Organizer (*www.familyorganizer.org)
by Dr. Brian Kluth and used with permission.

Appendix F

ASSETS AND POSSESSIONS

Periodically, it is wise to contemplate what material items have been entrusted to your care.

1. Determine the items that you have in your possession, and their market or resale value.
2. Contemplate deeply and honestly to determine which of these items you need and are actually using.
3. Are there any items that could be passed along to someone you know who could benefit from their use?
4. Are there any items that should be sold?
5. Are there any items (in the near future or after your funeral) that could be given to benefit the religious institution or nonprofit organization of your choice?

Visit www.idonate.com if you want to donate some of these assets to a church, charity, religious or nonprofit organization.

Important note: It is wise to discuss with your religious institution or nonprofit organization the best way to donate an asset to them. Depending on the value and type of asset, it may be wise to have the organization assist you in obtaining the help of an experienced estate planning professional to determine how to most effectively and affordably "transfer" an asset. Careful planning with experienced professional counsel versed in evaluating tax and estate planning issues will maximize the value of this gift to a nonprofit, to yourself and to your family.

"From what you have, take an offering for the LORD. Everyone who is willing is to bring to the LORD an offering of gold, silver, and bronze."
—Exodus 35:4–5

✓	List of Assets You Have In Your Possession	Estimated Value as of (date) _____	Details, descriptions, or specific desires for these items. If applicable, identify any item(s) you feel God would like you to give to a ministry or nonprofit now or in the future (i.e., sell the item and give the cash proceeds OR donate the specific item to a ministry or nonprofit to use or sell).
	Vehicle		
	Vehicle		
	Checking Account(s) and Cash		
	CD's/Savings Accounts		
	Motorcycles/Recreational Vehicles		
	Motor Home/RV/Trailer/Camper		
	Boats/Watercraft and Equipment		
	Home		
	Timeshare, Condo, Vacation Property		
	Sports/Exercise/Hunting Equipment		
	Workshop or Garage Tools/Equipment		
	Craft or Camera Equipment/Supplies		
	Musical Instruments		
	Appliances/Furniture/Furnishings		
	Jewelry/Gems/Furs		
	Antiques/Art/Memorabilia/Heirlooms		
	Books/Videos/Albums		
	China/Crystal/Glassware/Silver/etc.		
	Stocks/Bonds/Mutual funds/CDs		

	US Notes/Bills/Bonds		
	Commodities		
	Pension Funds (Employer or Military)		
	Retirement Accounts		
	College Savings Funds		
	Collections (Coins/Stamps/Crafts/Toys)		
	Trust Fund(s) or Inheritance Funds		
	Rental Properties		
	Business, Farm, Ranch: Buildings/Land		
	Business Vehicles/Equipment/Supplies		
	Undeveloped Land or Farmland		
	Livestock/Animals		
	Possessions in Storage Units		
	Foundation or Donor-Advised Funds		
	Business Partnerships/Ownership		
	Real Estate Partnerships		

From *Family Organizer (*www.familyorganizer.org)
by Dr. Brian Kluth and used with permission.

Appendix G
FAMILY MEDICAL INFORMATION

Health Insurance Company _____

Policy # _____Telephone _____

Location of insurance cards (wallet/s, desk drawer or?) _____

Medicaid/Medicare info _____

Location of organ donor card/instructions/permissions _____

Prescriptions: Dental _____

Prescriptions: Vision _____

Doctors/Dentists:

Name _____Specialty _____Telephone _____

Name _____Specialty _____Telephone_____

Name _____Specialty _____Telephone _____

Name _____Specialty _____Telephone_____

Medical History: Names of family member/relative and approximate age at time of diagnosis (if known)

Heart disease _____

Stroke _____

Cancer (specific type/s) _____

Depression/suicide _____

Diabetes _____

High cholesterol _____

High blood pressure _____

Miscarriages _____

Infant/childhood deaths _____

Allergies _____

Amputations (reason) _____

Other _____

Immunization History: Write date(s) immunizations given (if known)

Hepatitis A _____

Hepatitis B _____

Influenza _____

MMR _____

Pneumonia _____

Meningitis _____

Tetanus _____

Chicken pox _____

Major Surgeries: Write type of surgery, year and/or approximate age at the time of surgery (if known)

_____

_____

_____

_____

Prescriptions: Write doctor's name, name of medication, reason for medication (if known)

_____

_____

_____

_____

From *Family Organizer* (www.familyorganizer.org)

by Dr. Brian Kluth and used with permission.

PRETIREMENT GLOSSARY

401(k) — a type of retirement savings account that serves as an alternative to the traditional retirement pension, which was paid by employers. Employer contributions with the 401(k) can vary, but in general the 401(k) had the effect of shifting the burden for retirement savings to workers themselves.

Advance Medical Directive — instructions given by individuals specifying what actions should be taken for their health in the event that they are no longer able to make decisions due to illness or incapacity. Another person is appointed to make such decisions on their behalf.

All in Trust Until a Certain Age — a trust in which a child receives a smaller amount. It holds the child's share in a trust, protecting the assets from squandering and mismanagement by the child, and when the child reaches a stated age, it is simply distributed to the child outright, free of trust.

Annuity — an income stream generated when an insured party, usually an individual, pays a life insurance company a single premium that will later be distributed back to the insured party over time. They traditionally provide a guaranteed distribution of income over time, until the death of the person or persons named in the contract or until a final date, whichever comes first.

Beneficiary — the recipient who benefits from the distribution of funds, an estate or other benefits.

Bequest — a gift of personal property by will.

Blue Chip Industry — a large, national company with a strong record of stable earnings and dividend growth. A company with a very high quality reputation for management and products.

Certificate of Deposit (CD) — interest-bearing instrument offered by banks. CDs offer higher rates of return than most comparable investments while the invested money is tied up until the certificate's maturation date. Money removed before maturity will be penalized. CDs are low risk, low return investments, and are also known as "time deposits," because the account holder has agreed to keep the money in the account for a specified amount of time, anywhere from three months to six years.

Chartered Federal Employee Benefits Consultant (ChFEBC) — financial professionals who are required to stay up to date on the ever-changing federal government benefits programs and maintain extensive knowledge about FERS, CSRS, and Special Provisions.

Charitable Gift — this plan provides a federal income tax deduction in the year that the annuity is entered. The amount of the gift is determined by the age of the annuitant, the annuity rate, and the principal amount. Another advantage of the gift annuity is that part of the annual income is considered tax-exempt.

Charitable Lead Trust — a charitable gift in which the person creates a trust to provide current income to a charitable organization for a specified period of time (5, 10, 15, or more years). At the end of that time the assets of the trust are returned to family members. The charitable lead trust may help wealthy families transfer assets to heirs with little or no estate or gift tax.

Charitable Remainder Unitrust — designed for the person who wants to make a gift to a charitable organization, but needs income during life. This trust is especially suited for a person with highly appreciated property (either securities or real estate). It is possible to transfer the property to the trust and avoid all tax on capital gain.

Common Trust — if you have two or more children and at least one child is under age 25 or so, you may prefer to hold all of the assets in one, single trust until the youngest child attains, say, age 25. This trust (called a "common trust") will allow the education expenses of younger children to be paid before you divide your property into separate shares for each child.

Community Spouse — when a married couple applies for Medicaid, this term refers to the spouse who is still residing in the community.

Community Spouse Resource Allowance (CSRA) — a Medicaid term that refers to the "protected amount" of assets a Community Spouse is allowed to own that does not count against the $2,000 that the Nursing Home Spouse is permitted to own.

Corporate Personal Representative — there are many independent trust companies or trust departments of banks (known as "corporate fiduciaries") with powers under state law to manage estates and trusts.

Court Order of Support — a local court order that sets forth the amount of income that the Nursing Home Spouse must pay each month to the Community Spouse if their monthly income is insufficient. This Order must be recognized by the Medicaid agency.

Certified Senior Advisor (CSA) — a professional who has knowledge about aging and the important health, financial, and social issues that affect the majority of retirees.

Civil Service Retirement System (CSRS) — a defined-benefit plan, similar to a pension, that provides retirement, disability and survivor benefits for most civilian employees in the U.S. federal government. Upon the creation of a new Federal Employees Retirement System (FERS) in 1987, those newly hired after that date cannot participate in CSRS. CSRS continues to provide retirement benefits to those eligible to receive them.

Durable Power of Attorney for Health Care — a document authorizing another to act as one's agent or attorney, especially in the event that a patient has been incapacitated. This document may give the agent authorization to use the patient's funds to pay bills, contract for hospice services for the patient's care, and also make basic health care decisions for the patient.

Entitlement Programs — government programs designed to help the elderly, ill and unemployed citizens. Medicare and Medicaid fall under this classification.

Estate Planning — the process of planning your estate in such a way that after you die, it properly affects the people in your life, transfers your property efficiently while minimizing probate and tax expense, and guides those who will assist you in achieving your goals. It involves the right legal documents that will direct those in the process of settling your estate.

Fair Hearing — an administrative appeal within the Medicaid state agency that makes the determination of financial eligibility for Medicaid.

Family Allowance — Medicaid term in which an additional amount may be deducted from the Nursing Home Spouse's income before paying the nursing home, if certain other family members are living in the home with the Community Spouse. For these purposes, the term "family member" only includes minor or dependent children, dependent parents, or dependent siblings of the Nursing Home Spouse or of the Community Spouse who are residing with the Community Spouse.

Federal Employees Retirement System (FERS) — a three-tiered retirement system for government employees with a smaller defined benefit (pension), Social Security, and a 401(k)-style system called the Thrift Savings Plan (TSP). Replaced the CSRS in the 1980s.

Fixed Index Annuity (FIA) — a contract in which you have the option to make either a lump sum contribution or a series of contributions, which in turn will pay a guaranteed rate of interest for a set period of time. Both the principal and interest are guaranteed, and you'll face a penalty for early withdrawal.

Gift Annuity Agreement or Deferred Gift Annuity Agreement — a charitable gift that allows a person to make a future gift and receive a guaranteed stream of income for life. Annuity rates are based on age, and often are quite competitive with what a person can earn from low risk investments in the market. A deferred payment annuity allows for payments to begin at a later date (such as at retirement), and results in both a larger charitable gift and a greater annual income.

Guardian — a person or persons who will make personal and financial decisions for any of your minor children, if you are no longer living or are incapacitated and can no longer take care of them. Without a will, the court could pick whomever they want, and your wishes would never be known. Although the local probate court actually appoints the Guardians, the court almost always appoints the person(s) named in the parent's will.

Health Insurance Portability and Accountability Act (HIPPA) — a U.S. law designed to provide privacy standards to protect patients' medical records and other health information provided to health plans, doctors, hospitals and other health care providers.

Home and Community Based Services (HCBS) — provides certain kinds of Medicaid assistance to elderly people, outside the nursing home. In-home services include: case management, personal care services, respite care services (i.e., care for the patient in a nursing home for a few days, to give the home caregiver a needed break), adult day health services, homemaker/home health aide services, and habilitation (i.e., assisting people in furthering their skills in the areas of mobility, social behaviors, self care, basic safety, housekeeping, personal hygiene, health care, and financial management).

Immediate Annuity — a specially structured investment that allows a person to convert a sum of money into a guaranteed series of payments over a fixed term and begins after purchase.

Income-Cap States (Medicare) — some states do not have a medically needy program serving nursing home residents. In these states, individuals are not permitted to spend down their assets to the Social Security income level, or cap, to become eligible for Medicaid-covered nursing home care. Income-cap states are Alabama, Alaska, Colorado, Delaware, Idaho, Mississippi, Nevada, New Mexico, Ohio, South Dakota and Wyoming.

Individual Retirement Account (IRA) — a personal, tax-deferred investor-established account set up to hold and invest funds until retirement. Contributions are often tax-deductible, but they are taxed as ordinary income when withdrawn.

Life Estate Gift — a person may deed a personal residence, farm, or other real property to a charitable organization now, but retain lifetime enjoyment and use of the property. The person may continue to live in the home. In the case of other property, the person may continue to collect any income generated. The person continues to pay the taxes, insurance, and maintenance of the property. At the person's death, the property becomes the immediate property of the church, ministry, or charity.

Life Insurance Gifts — a method of contributing to charity by taking out life insurance on yourself with the charity as a beneficiary

Lifetime Trust — this is recommended for larger estates, if a child's share will be over $300,000. It protects the child's share from divorce, lawsuits, and creditors of the child, and excludes the property from the child's taxable estate.

Living Trust — an estate planning tool that could be a good alternative to a will. Such a trust can be written to include a charitable bequest, just like in a will. Assets in the trust are distributed according to the terms of the trust and do not pass through the probate process.

Living Will — a document in which a person specifies which life-prolonging measures he or she does, and does not, want to be taken if he or she becomes terminally ill or incapacitated.

Long Term Care (LTC) Insurance — this insurance policy pays some or all costs of nursing home care for those who quality. Premiums are based on the applicant's age and are expected to remain stable for the life of the policy. When the policyholder qualifies for long term care, premium payments stop. Qualifications include: medical necessity, cognitive impairment and inability to carry our certain activities of daily living.

Look-back Period — a period of five years from the date when a Medicaid applicant last gave a gift to the day he or she is permitted to apply for Medicaid.

Medicaid — a program, funded by the federal and state governments, that pays for medical care for those who can't afford it. It generally provides for low-income individuals or families, as well as the elderly and disabled. Applicants must meet certain requirements, including income level. Each state manages their own Medicaid program and is able to set their own requirements and other guidelines.

Medicare — the popular name for the federal health insurance program for those who have turned age 65 or become disabled.

Minimum Monthly Maintenance Needs Allowance (MMMNA) — Medicaid permits the Community Spouse to retain a certain portion of the institutionalized spouse's income to bring the Community Spouse's income up to the minimum monthly maintenance needs allowance. This is calculated at $1,821 per month minus the Community Spouse's other income. State laws vary.

Modified Endowment Life Insurance — a type of life insurance that is payable to the insured if he or she is still living on the policy's maturity date. The monies go to a beneficiary otherwise. There are MECs that have long term care riders on them so one can use the death benefit in a nursing home and whatever is left over becomes a death benefit like an insurance product.

Monthly Income Allowance (MIA) — a Medicaid term referring to the maximum amount a community spouse is permitted to receive. If the community spouse has income that is less than the MIA, income may be contributed by the Nursing Home Spouse, if available, to bring the community spouse's income up to the current allowance

Municipal Bond — a bond issued by a state, city, or local government. Municipalities issue bonds to raise capital for their day-to-day activities and for specific projects that they might be undertaking. Interest on municipal bonds is generally exempt from federal tax and from most state and local taxes, especially if you live in the state in which the bond is issued.

Nursing Home Spouse — when a married couple is applying for Medicaid, this term refers to the spouse residing in a nursing home.

Omnibus Reconciliation Act (OBRA) — part of this act was the establishment of estate recovery of assets for those who become eligible for Medicaid. This new law demanded that all states engage in estate recovery, and, since then, all states have passed laws that enable the state to place a lien on the home of those who qualify for Medicaid. Many of these states place liens on property for Medicaid recovery during the process of convalescence.

Pay on Death (or POD) Account — some institutions may refer to this arrangement as Transfer on Death (or TOD). These arrangements allow for the assets to pass directly to the named beneficiary, often a charitable organization, and avoid the probate process.

Personal Representative — the person or company appointed by the court to supervise the administration of your estate. Without a will, the court picks the representative; your wishes may never be known. Only with your will can you ensure that the person you want is put in charge of your assets.

Power of Attorney — a document that gives someone (called your "Agent") the legal authority to make decisions for you financially and carry out your wishes. This would typically apply if you became incapacitated and therefore unable to make these decisions yourself.

Pre-DRA Gifts/Post-DRA Gifts — the Deficit Reduction Act (DRA), effective February 8, 2006, modified the Federal Medicaid Act and significantly changed the strategies that were used before that date. Gifts made prior to February 2006 are considered pre-DRA and follow rules that were in place at that time. Any gifts made after that date are held to the post-DRA rules.

Prenuptial Agreement — a written agreement between two people planning to marry. It lists their assets and liabilities and lays out the ground rules for how each person's individual property will be divided should the marriage end. It also states how their earnings and savings will be used, and whether or not alimony will be paid. A common document for people who are earning large amounts of money, have large properties or have children from previous relationships.

PREtirement —the term being used to describe a new phase of life that fits between career and retirement. Traditionally our lives have been divided into three stages: education, career and retirement. But with longer life expectancies, generally better health and the economic need to continue to earn an income, the line between career and retirement is blurring. Emerging from that blur is an entirely new life stage called PREtirement.

Probate — a legal process that involves proving that the deceased's will is valid, identifying the deceased person's property and having it appraised, paying outstanding debts and taxes, and distributing the property per the will or state law.

Required Minimum Distribution (RMD) — the minimum amounts that a retirement plan account owner must withdraw annually starting with the year that he or she reaches 70½ years of age or, if later, the year in which he or she retires.

Retroactive Coverage — it is possible to apply for Medicaid coverage for a period beginning up to three months prior to the date of application. If the applicant would have qualified for Medicaid as of such date had he or she applied at such time, then the applicant will be covered starting on such date.

Reverse Mortgage — a non-recourse loan with no credit qualification and no need to pay the money back. A mortgage company will provide you with either a lump sum for your home or an income stream based upon the value of your home. The reverse mortgage company cannot kick you out of the home. You can use the money for an annuity or long term care premiums. The mortgage company simply will sell the home upon the death of the second spouse and they'll recover the money they provided you (plus interest and fees as their profit). Any amount left over after the sale will go to your chosen beneficiaries.

Revocable Living Trust — an arrangement made for the management and distribution of your property. Like a will, the trust is revocable, meaning that you can modify it at any time. They are established by a written agreement that appoints a "trustee" to administer the property, and gives detailed instructions on how the property is to be managed and eventually distributed.

Social Security — established by the Social Security Act of 1935, this program is designed to provide income to seniors and the disabled. Funded by taxes levied on employees, employers, and the self-employed, Social Security income is based on lifetime earnings and available when you either become disabled or reach the federally mandated age of retirement, which depends on when you were born.

Snapshot Rule — a Medicaid term in which the CSRA is based on the value of the couple's assets as of the date the Nursing Home Spouse first entered the nursing home. To be precise, this "snapshot" is taken on the first day of the month in which the Nursing Home Spouse is in the nursing home (or a patient in the hospital just prior to entering the nursing home, as the case may be) and likely to remain there for a continuous period of at least 30 consecutive days.

Special Needs Trust For a Disabled Child — a trust in which the trust assets may only be used to supplement and not replace any benefits that are otherwise available to your child from any governmental source, such as SSI, Medicaid or Social Security.

Spend-down States (Medicare) — some states have medically needy programs for people who would qualify for Medicaid categorically, but are "over income." These persons can "spend down" to the Medicaid level by deducting incurred medical expenses. Spend-down states are California, Connecticut, Georgia, Hawaii, Illinois, Kentucky, Maine, Maryland, Massachusetts, New Hampshire, New Jersey, New York, North Carolina, North Dakota, Pennsylvania, Rhode Island, South Carolina, Tennessee, Vermont, Virginia, Washington, West Virginia, and Wisconsin. Washington, DC also falls into this category.

Staggered Distributions — a trust in which distributions of one-third of the trust are made outright to the child at a stated age, half the balance five years later, and the full balance five years after that.

Successor Personal Representative — a person who will replace your initial Personal Representative(s) if for any reason the initial Personal Representative(s) fails or ceases to serve. For example, the Personal Representative(s) may decline to serve, or resign, become ill, or get removed by the beneficiaries (or the court) at some point in the future.

Successor Trustee — a person or persons who will replace your initial Trustee(s) if for any reason the initial Trustee(s) fails or ceases to serve. For example, the Trustee(s) may decline to serve, or resign, become ill, or get removed by the beneficiaries (or the court) at some point in the future.

Tax Exempt Securities — a security in which the income produced is free from federal, state and local taxes. Most come in the form of municipal bonds. U.S. savings bond interest may also be free from federal income taxes.

Trustee — a person or company named in your will (or living trust), to manage, invest, and distribute the assets held in the trust(s) created inside your will (or living trust).

Will — a legal document in which a person specifies how his or her estate will be managed and distributed after his or her death. It must be probated in most states.

HELPFUL INTERNET RESOURCES FOR RETIREES, AGING ADULTS, AND CAREGIVERS

Because I Love You Christian Planning Guide: **www.MyFamilyForms.org**. 30-plus pages of valuable resources, checklists and forms for spiritual matters, finances, household information, documents, family tree, life legacy, funeral plans, wealth sharing/distribution, aging parents, child guardians, estate planning and more.

Christian Retirees with RVs — Volunteer Service Opportunities: **www.workersonwheels.com**, **www.mmap.org**, **www.sowerministry.org**, **www.rvics.com**, **www.habitat.org/gv/rv.html**

Christian Volunteer Opportunities for Retirees: **www.finishers.org**, **www.servantopportunities.net**

Kingdom Quest Christian Website: **www.kingdomquest.com/seniors.html**. Links to 100 senior websites.

5 Wishes Booklet: **www.agingwithdignity.org**. A valuable "fill-in-the-blank" document to communicate your near-the-end-of-life medical, personal, emotional and spiritual wishes for family and medical staff/professionals.

American Association of Retired Persons: **www.aarp.org**

Administration on Aging: **www.aoa.gov**

Aging Parents and Elder Care: **www.aging-parents-and-elder-care.com**. Excellent source for valuable articles, checklists, referrals and website links.

Alzheimer's Association: **www.alz.org**

Assisted Living Info: **www.assistedlivinginfo.com**. Online guide for selecting an assisted living facility, retirement community, or other personal care facility anywhere in the United States.

Be Seen and Heard — Danette Kubanda Media & PR: **www.DanetteKubanda. com.** Media coaching and consulting, writing, editing, social media and publicity services.

Benefits Checkup: **www.benefitscheckup.org**. Helps you find and enroll in federal, state, local and private programs that help pay for prescription drugs, utility bills, meals, health care and other needs.

Caregiving website: **www.caregiving.com**

Center for Medicaid and Medicare Services: **www.cms.hhs.gov** . Valuable online help and answers.

Center for Medicare Advocacy: **www.medicareadvocacy.org**. Nonprofit organization which provides education, advocacy, and legal assistance to help elders and people with disabilities obtain necessary healthcare.

Children of Aging Parents Association: **www.caps4caregivers.org**. A nonprofit organization serving caregivers of the elderly or chronically ill with reliable information, referrals and support.

Christian Association of Senior Adults: **www.gocasa.org**

Drugs.com: **www.drugs.com**. Comprehensive information on more than 24,000 different drugs and medicines.

Eldercare Locator: **www.eldercare.gov**

Family Caregiver Alliance: **www.caregiver.org**

Focus on the Family: **www.family.org.** Valuable articles, resources and referrals from a Christian perspective.

Government Senior Citizens Resources: **www.seniors.gov**

Health Assistance Partnership: **www.healthassistancepartnership.org**. Information about the needs of Medicaid and Medicare beneficiaries, commercially insured consumers, and the uninsured.

Mayo Clinic: **www.mayoclinic.com**. Health and wellness information from the Mayo clinic.

Medicare: **www.medicare.gov** . The official U.S. site for people with Medicare. Information about nursing homes, physicians, benefits, and coverage questions.

National Alliance for Caregiving: **www.caregiving.org**

National Family Caregivers Association: **www.nfcacares.org**

National Association of Professional Geriatric Care Managers: **www.caremanager.org**. Online referral service.

Nursing Home Information: **www.nursinghomeinfo.com** . Information about choosing a nursing home, listings of facilities and a needs assessment tool.

Senior Net: **www.seniornet.org**. Provides older adults education for and access to computer technologies.

Social Security Administration: **www.socialsecurity.gov**

Solutions for Better Aging: **www.agenet.com**. Articles, online tools and checklists on caregiving, housing, legal, insurance, health, drugs and home.

Stop Trading Your Time for Money: **www.StefanieHartman.com** or **www.MITProgram.com**. Private or group coaching on how to create NEW income and creating your Second Act while staying at home—for baby boomers and retirees.

Web MD: **www.webmd.com**. Online medical information and advice.

Well Spouse Foundation: **www.wellspouse.org**. Support for partners of the chronically ill and/or disabled.

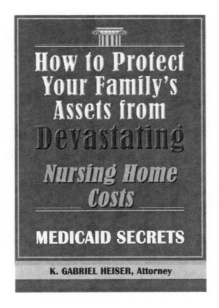

Are You Ready for PREtirement?

90 Days to Build the Secure, Happy Retirement of Your Dreams

Did you know…

- Seventy percent of people over age 65 will end up in a convalescent rehabilitation center? And that 20 percent of those *under* 65 may need a convalescent stay at some point in their lives?
- Care in a nursing home costs on average $200 to $500 a day, and to qualify for Medicaid assistance to pay for nursing home care, you may be required to spend down your assets to extremely low levels?
- Unless you designate someone to speak for you should you become incapacitated, your doctor, or the bank, or your closest living relative will be forced to make choices on your behalf—choices that may have nothing to do with your wishes?
- If you have even a very small amount of assets or property, your estate may have to go through probate when you die? And probate can take years and cost tens of thousands of dollars of the money you wanted to pass to your heirs?

PREparing for your future retirement doesn't have to be difficult or overwhelming. Let PREtirement expert Kris Miller show you how to PREpare for a great future by Planning Retirement Early!

In this dynamic, interactive course, Kris Miller uses her 21-plus years of experience to walk you through the process of creating and implementing a plan that will give you "estate of mind"—the peace of mind that comes when all your personal and financial affairs are in order and you know you'll have the money to care for all your retirement needs.

You will learn how to...

- Find risk-free investments that will provide secure returns in *any* market
- Avoid the devastating financial impact of nursing home or convalescent care costs
- Deal successfully with government programs such as Medicare and Social Security
- Create a plan that will pass your estate to your heirs without probate
- Choose the best legal and financial representatives to speak for you when you cannot
- Organize your affairs and communicate your wishes to your family and representatives, creating peace of mind both for you and for them
- Enjoy your retirement because you know these important issues have been handled!

The secrets Kris Miller reveals in this course are usually only known to attorneys, specialists in elder care, health care advocates, benefits administrators, and other retirement experts. But with Kris Miller's simple system and her clear instruction and coaching, you too will become the master of your own retirement future.

No one should have to spend their "golden years" worrying about money or concerned that they'll be a burden on their children because of health or financial issues. Everyone should be able to live a happy senior life and pass their estate to their heirs worry-free when the time comes. Let Kris Miller's 90-day course show you how!

Receive a 20 percent discount! Go to:

www.ReadyForPREtirement.com/AreYouReadyforPREtirement

and enter coupon code READY20

PREtirement
Inn Retirement Early

Enroll in Kris's FREE teleseminar series

PREtirement Masters

www.ReadyforPREtirement.com/teleseminars

In these valuable, enlightening and inspiring sessions, including interviews with other retirement experts, Kris will share secrets and tips for handling every aspect of planning for a happy, secure future. Learn how to live worry-free in your "golden years" because you have PREpared for PREtirement!

Enroll Today! Visit

www.PREtirementMasters.com

CPSIA information can be obtained at www.ICGtesting.com
Printed in the USA
LVOW061628230712

291212LV00010B/101/P